Old Testament Theology

BIBLIOGRAPHIES

Tremper Longman III
General Editor and Old Testament Editor

Craig A. Evans
New Testament Editor

1. Pentateuch
2. Historical Books
3. Poetry and Wisdom
4. Prophecy and Apocalyptic
5. Jesus
6. Synoptic Gospels
7. Johannine Writings
8. Luke–Acts
9. Pauline Writings
10. Hebrews and General Epistles
11. Old Testament Introduction
12. New Testament Introduction
13. Old Testament Theology
14. New Testament Theology

BIBLIOGRAPHIES No. 13

Old Testament Theology

Elmer A. Martens

Baker Books

A Division of Baker Book House Co
Grand Rapids, Michigan 49516

© 1997 by Elmer A. Martens

Published by Baker Books
a division of Baker Book House Company
P.O. Box 6287, Grand Rapids, MI 49516-6287

Printed in the United States of America

Library of Congress Cataloging-in-Publication Data

Martens, E. A.
    Old Testament theology / Elmer A. Martens.
        p.   cm. — (IBR bibliographies : no. 13)
    Includes bibliographical references and index.
    ISBN 0-8010-2146-4 (pbk.)
        1. Bible. O.T.—Theology—Bibliography. 2. Bible. O.T.—
Bibliography. I. Title. II. Series.
Z7772.A1M37   1997
[BS1192.5]
016.221—dc21   97-34326

For information about academic books, resources for Christian leaders, and all new
releases available from Baker Book House, visit our web site:
http://www.bakerbooks.com

Contents

Series Preface   7
Acknowledgments   9
Abbreviations   11

1.   REFERENCE WORKS   14
1.1   Indexing and Abstracting Sources   14
1.2   Encyclopedias and Dictionaries   17
1.3   Theological Dictionaries and Word Books   19
2.   SERIAL LITERATURE   23
2.1   Journals   23
2.2   Monograph Series   24
2.3   Collected Essays   25
3.   HISTORY OF THE DISCIPLINE/STATE OF THE
      DISCIPLINE   30
4.   ISSUES IN THE DISCIPLINE   37
4.1   The Task of Old Testament Theology   37
4.2   Biblical Theology and Other Disciplines   42
4.3   Method of Old Testament Theology   45
4.4   History and Faith   50
4.5   The Place of Wisdom   54
4.6   Center/Unity   56
5.   PERSPECTIVES ON OLD TESTAMENT THEOLOGY   61
5.1   Biblical Theology: Canon, Old Testament, New Testament   61
5.2   The Jewish Perspective   67
5.3   Sociological Perspectives   68
5.4   Christian Preaching   69
6.   OLD TESTAMENT THEOLOGIES   73
7.   THEOLOGIES OF CORPORA   88
7.1   Pentateuch and Pentateuchal Sources   88
7.2   Former Prophets/Deuteronomic History   90
7.3   Latter Prophets   90

7.4   Poetry   91
7.5   Wisdom   91
7.6   Period Theologies   93
8.   THEOLOGIES: BOOK BY BOOK   94
8.1   Methodology   95
8.2   Compendia   95
8.3   Books of the Old Testament   96
9.   MONOGRAPHS ON SELECTED BIBLICAL THEMES   111
9.1   Anger   111
9.2   Anthropology   111
9.3   Apocalyptic   112
9.4   Blessing   113
9.5   Covenant   113
9.6   Creation   115
9.7   Cult/Worship   117
9.8   Death/Resurrection   117
9.9   Eschatology   118
9.10   Ethics   119
9.11   Faith   120
9.12   God/Yahweh   120
9.13   Grace/Faith/Faithfulness   122
9.14   Healing/Health   122
9.15   Justice/Righteousness/Holiness   123
9.16   Kingdom of God/Kingship   123
9.17   Land   124
9.18   Law   125
9.19   Messiah   125
9.20   Mission   126
9.21   Peace   127
9.22   Prayer   127
9.23   Providence   128
9.24   Righteousness   128
9.25   Sacrifice   128
9.26   Salvation   129
9.27   Sin   129
9.28   Spirit of God/Spirituality   129
9.29   War/Peace   130
9.30   Worship   131

Index of Modern Authors   133

Series Preface

With the proliferation of journals and publishing houses dedicated to biblical studies, it has become impossible for even the most dedicated scholar to keep in touch with the vast materials now available for research in all the different parts of the canon. How much more difficult for the minister, rabbi, student, or interested layperson! Herein lies the importance of bibliographies and in particular this series—IBR Bibliographies.

Bibliographies help guide students to works relevant to their research interests. They cut down the time needed to locate materials, thus providing the researcher with more time to read, assimilate, and write. These benefits are especially true for the IBR Bibliographies. First, the series is conveniently laid out along the major divisions of the canon, with four volumes planned on the Old Testament, six on the New Testament, and four on methodology (see page 2). Each volume will contain approximately five hundred entries, arranged under various topics to allow for ease of reference. Since the possible entries far exceed this number, the compiler of each volume must select the more important and helpful works for inclusion. Furthermore, the entries are briefly annotated in order to inform the reader about their contents more specifically, once again giving guidance to the appropriate material and saving time by preventing the all too typical "wild goose chase" in the library.

One of the problems with published bibliographies in the past is that they are soon out of date. The development of computer-based publishing has changed this, however, and it is the plan of the Institute for Biblical Research and Baker Book House to publish updates of each volume about every five years.

Since the series is designed primarily for American and British students, the emphasis is on works written in English, with a five-percent limit on titles not translated into English. Fortunately, a number of the most important foreign-language works have been translated into English, and wherever this is the case this information is included along with the original publication data. Again keeping in mind the needs of the student, we have decided to list the English translation before the original title, and in this volume the titles are arranged for the most part according to the appearance of the English translations.

These bibliographies are presented under the sponsorship of the Institute for Biblical Research (IBR), an organization of evangelical Christian scholars with specialties in both Old and New Testaments and their ancillary disciplines. The IBR has met annually since 1970; its name and constitution were adopted in 1973. Besides its annual meetings (normally held the evening and morning prior to the annual meeting of the Society of Biblical Literature), the institute publishes a journal, *Bulletin for Biblical Research,* and conducts regional study groups on various biblical themes in several areas of the United States and Canada. The Institute for Biblical Research encourages and fosters scholarly research among its members, all of whom are at a level to qualify for a university lectureship. Finally, the IBR and the series editor extend their thanks to Baker Book House for its efforts to bring this series to publication. In particular, we would like to thank David Aiken for his wise guidance in giving shape to the project.

Tremper Longman III
Westminster Theological Seminary

Acknowledgments

Help in preparing this bibliography has come to me from several special persons. I mention with gratitude the Fellows of the American College of Biblical Theologians, who offered suggestions on categorization and selection. To Professor Thomas McComiskey, founder, but taken from us by death in March 1996, I dedicate this work in memoriam.

To Keith Wells, Reference Librarian at Rolfing Library, Trinity International University, Deerfield, Illinois, I owe a special debt for his helpful suggestions and his interest in this project. Two teaching assistants, George Klassen and Ken Peters, were helpful in the early stages. Professors John Sailhamer and H. Kent Richards as well as Bill Tooman made valuable suggestions. Dr. Tremper Longman, general editor for the series, gave helpful counsel. Maria denBoer, copy editor at Baker, was patient and professional. Of printed sources, the *Book List* of the Society for Old Testament Study and *Old Testament Abstracts* have been a particular boon.

Given a free schedule and a family widely scattered I benefited much from libraries across the country. I mention them, as well as their library staffs, with much appreciation. In addition to Rolfing Library, Deerfield, Illinois, I gratefully recognize the libraries at Southwestern Baptist Seminary, Fort Worth, Texas; the Denver Seminary, Denver, Colorado; the Ira J. Taylor Library and its reference librarian, Paul Millette, at Iliff School of Theology, Denver, Colorado; Turpin Library, Dallas Theological Seminary, Dallas, Texas; Catholic University of America, Washington, D.C.; Feehan Memorial Library, University of

St. Mary-on-the-Lake, Mundelein, Illinois; the Flora Lamson Hewlett Library at the Graduate Theological Union, Berkeley, California; and the Hiebert Library at my home institution in Fresno, California, and Anne Guenther, its reference librarian.

Elmer A. Martens
Mennonite Brethren Biblical Seminary
Fresno, California
October 1996

Abbreviations

ABD	*Anchor Bible Dictionary*
AUSS	*Andrews University Seminary Studies*
BBR	*Bulletin for Biblical Research*
BCE	*Before the Christian Era*
Bib	*Biblica*
BibSac	*Bibliotheca Sacra*
BJRL	*Bulletin of the John Rylands University Library of Manchester*
BTB	*Biblical Theology Bulletin*
BV	*Biblical Viewpoint*
BZAW	Beiheftezur zeitschrift für die alt-testamentliche Wissenschaft
CBQ	*Catholic Biblical Quarterly*
CurTM	*Currents in Theology and Mission*
EAJT	*East Asian Journal of Theology*
EOTH	*Essays on Old Testament Hermeneutics* (see #43)
EQ	*Evangelical Quarterly*
ET	*Expository Times*
EvTh	*Evangelische Theologie*
ExpTim	*Expository Times*
FOTT	*The Flowering of Old Testament Theology* (see #54)
HBT	*Horizons in Biblical Theology*
HTR	*Harvard Theological Review*
IDB	*Interpreter's Dictionary of the Bible*
IDBS	*Interpreter's Dictionary of the Bible Supplementary Volume*

Int	*Interpretation*
IEPLOT	*An Index to English Periodical Literature on the Old Testament and Ancient Near Eastern Studies*
ISBE	*International Standard Bible Encyclopedia*
IZBG	*Internationale Zeitschriftenschau für Bibelwissenschaft und Grenzgebiete*
JAAR	*Journal of the American Academy of Religion*
JBTh	*Jahrbuch für Biblische Theologie*
JETS	*Journal of the Evangelical Theological Society*
JR	*Journal of Religion*
JSOT	*Journal for the Study of the Old Testament*
JSOTSup	Journal for the Study of the Old Testament Supplement Series
JTS	*Journal of Theological Studies*
NICOT	New International Commentary on the Old Testament
NIDNTT	*New International Dictionary of New Testament Theology*
NIDOTTE	*New International Dictionary of Old Testament Theology and Exegesis*
NSBT	New Studies in Biblical Theology
OBT	Overtures to Biblical Theology (series)
OTA	*Old Testament Abstracts*
OTCF	*The Old Testament and Christian Faith* (see #42)
OTE	*Old Testament Essays*
OTG	Old Testament Guides (series)
RevExp	*Review and Expositor*
RGG	*Religion in Geschichte und Gegenwart*
SBS	*Stuttgarter Bibelstudien*
SBT	Studies in Biblical Theology (series)
SJOT	*Scandinavian Journal of the Old Testament*
SJT	*Scottish Journal of Theology*
SOTBT	Studies in Old Testament Biblical Theology (series)
SWJT	*Southwestern Journal of Theology*
TD	*Theology Digest*
TDNT	*Theological Dictionary of the New Testament*
TDOT	*Theological Dictionary of the Old Testament*
ThR	*Theologische Rundschau*
ThSt	*Theologische Studien*
ThZ	*Theologische Zeitschrift*
TLZ	*Theologische Literaturzeitung*

TrinJ	*Trinity Journal*
TRZ	*Theologische Realenzyklopaedie*
TT	*Theology Today*
TWOT	*Theological Wordbook of the Old Testament*
TynBul	*Tyndale Bulletin*
TZ	*Theologische Zeitschrift*
VT	*Vetus Testamentum*
WBC	*Word Biblical Commentary*
WMANT	Wissenschaftliche Monographien zum Alten und Neuen Testament (series)
WTJ	*Westminster Theological Journal*
WuD	*Wort und Dienst*
ZAW	*Zeitschrift für die alttestamentliche Wissenschaft*
ZTK	*Zeitschrift für Theologie und Kirche*

1

Reference Works

As a formal discipline, biblical theology has more than two hundred years of history. Overviews of the discipline can be found in dictionaries and encyclopedias. This section lists these as well as other basic research tools.

An operating definition of the discipline comes from John Goldingay: "Biblical Theology seeks to express the content of the biblical faith, its structure and its component parts in their dynamic interrelationship in the Bible's own terms and according to its priorities" ("The Study of Old Testament Theology: Its Aims and Purposes," *TynBul* 26 [1975]: 39).

1.1 Indexing and Abstracting Sources

In addition to the listings below, certain monographs may be consulted for their extensive bibliographical listings: Reventlow (#213); Goldingay (#192); Hasel (#95); Reumann (#50); Ollenburger et al. (#54).

1   *The SOTS Book List*. An annual publication by the Society for Old Testament Study (London). H. H. Rowley, founding editor. 1946– . Cumulative volumes are published at various intervals. *Eleven Years of Bible Bibliography, 1946–1956*. Edited by H. H. Rowley for the Society for Old Testament Study. Indian Hills, Colo.: Falcon's Wing, 1957. *A Decade of Bible Bibliography, 1957–1966*. The book lists of the Society for Old Testament

Study, 1957–66. Edited by G. W. Anderson for the Society for Old Testament Study. Oxford: Blackwell, 1967. *Bible Bibliography, 1967–1973: Old Testament.* The book lists of the Society for Old Testament Study, 1967–73. Edited by P. R. Ackroyd. Oxford: Blackwell, 1974.

Lists only OT books—specifically, those published the preceding year throughout the world. Brief (150-word) critical reviews of each. One of the ten classifications is entitled "Law, Religion, and Theology." Author index. An indispensable resource.

2   *Internationale Zeitschriftenschau für Bibelwissenschaft und Grenzgebiete (IZBG) (International Review of Biblical Studies).* F. Stier, founding editor. Vol. 1 (1951–52). Stuttgart: Verlag Katholisches Bibelwerk. From volume 2 on, the publisher is Patmos Verlag in Düsseldorf.

Aspires to be a comprehensive index of books and articles. Brief abstracts are often in English but in German and French as well. Access to pertinent works in OT theology is best gained through the Contents under the section "Biblische Theologie," with categories such as OT/NT and "Altes Testament" (e.g., *Gott, Schöfung*). A standard, indispensable guide. Helpful for topics in OT theology.

3   *An Introductory Bibliography for the Study of Scripture.* Edited by G. S. Glanzman and J. A. Fitzmyer. Westminster, Md.: Newman, 1962. Revised Edition: J. A. Fitzmyer (ed.). Rome: Biblical Institute Press, 1981. Third Revised Edition: *Subsidia Biblical.* Vol. 3, 1990.

The first edition lists ten OT theologies with annotations (pp. 79–84). The revised edition has fourteen entries (pp. 92–95) with annotations, including information about book reviews on OT theologies. The third edition has been internationalized.

4   *Old Testament Abstracts (OTA).* Published thrice yearly by the Catholic Biblical Association. Managing editor at Catholic University of America, Washington, D.C. Bruce Vawter, first editor. 1978– .

Articles and books germane to OT theology may be found primarily in two sections: "Periodical Abstracts" and "Book Notices." A major tool for OT scholars since it draws on more than two hundred periodicals from many countries. Highly recommended; a great time-saver.

16   Old Testament Theology

5   *Theological and Religious Reference Materials.* G. E. Gorman and L. Gorman. Vol. 1: *General Resources and Biblical Studies.* Westport, Conn./London, 1984.

Annotations by the authors on OT theology are listed in the section "Biblical Studies: Handbooks," pp. 274–336.

6   *Elenchus of Biblica.* Edited by R. North. Rome: Pontifical Biblical Institute Press. Vol. 1 (1985). Vol. 8 (1992) was published in 1995. This new series follows *Elenchus Bibliographicus Biblicus,* which ceased publication with vol. 65, covering publications up through 1984.

Entries of articles from periodicals (some 1,200) and books in many languages with headings given in Latin and English. A valuable feature is the listing of book reviews. Access to pertinent material is via the Contents under "Theologia Biblica" with entries under topics (e.g., OT prayer) and also "General OT Biblical Theology." A required tool for extensive research.

7   *An Index to English Periodical Literature on the Old Testament and Ancient Near Eastern Studies (IEPLOT).* ATLA Bibliography Series, 21. Compiled and edited by W. G. Hupper. Metuchen, N.J., and London: The American Theological Library Association and Scarecrow. Vol. 1 (1987); Vol. 2 (1988); Vol. 3 (1990); Vol. 4 (1990); Vol. 5 (1992).

The sixth volume (1994), following a multiple-category schema of classification, treats category #3, "Critical Studies." Under the proposed schema (listed in 1:xxi) a volume(s) is projected on category #5, "Theological Studies Related to the Old Testament."

8   A. E. Zannoni. *The Old Testament: A Bibliography.* Old Testament Studies. Vol. 5. Collegeville, Minn.: Liturgical, 1992.

Entries primarily of books in the English language up through 1989. Intended as a functional guide for students, professional theologians, and ministers. The section on OT theology is found on pp. 197–227 and includes "Theologies of the Old Testament" and entries under "anthropology" and "various themes" (e.g., God, social justice, preaching). See also his section, "The World of the Old Testament." No annotations, but an index of names.

9   R. Dalman. "A Resource Guide for the Study of Basic Old Testament Theology." Electronic format. E-mail address: rdal man@undata.com

Intended to provide the core material for a course; evangelical in orientation. Centers primarily on the trinity, salvation, and revelation. Uneven treatment. Includes bibliography. Written in WordPerfect 5.1. Significant for its new medium.

1.2 Encyclopedias and Dictionaries

The listed articles are *about* the discipline of OT theology, and so offer orientation regarding its history, nature, and methodology. Some articles include brief summaries of OT theology by noted scholars.

10   J. Hempel. "Biblische Theologie und biblische Religionsgeschichte: I. AT." Pp. 1256b–59b in RGG^3, 1957.
Deals primarily with method (e.g., ANE comparison) and the relationship of the OT to NT (e.g., promise–fulfillment; typology). More of a history is given by H. Gunkel in RGG^2, 1927, pp. 1089–91.

11   K. Stendahl. "Biblical Theology, Contemporary." Pp. 418–32 in IDB^1, 1962. Reprinted as "Biblical Theology: A Program," in Stendahl's *Meanings: The Bible as Document and Guide*. Philadelphia: Fortress, 1984, pp. 11–44.
A highly influential essay by a Harvard professor who maintains that the function of biblical theology is descriptive. He notes the ramifications of such a position for both OT and NT, as well as for hermeneutics and preaching. Major bibliographical listing. Cf. in the same *IDB* volume the article by O. Betz, "Biblical Theology, History of," pp. 432–37. For a challenge to Stendahl, see B. C. Ollenburger, "What Krister Stendahl 'Meant'—A Normative Critique of 'Descriptive Biblical Theology,'" *HBT* 8 (1986): 61–98.

12   J. Barr. "Biblical Theology." Pp. 104–11 in *The Interpreter's Dictionary of the Bible Supplementary Volume (IDBS)*. Edited by K. Crim. Nashville: Abingdon, 1976.
Reviews biblical theology as a movement together with some themes associated with it (e.g., revelation in history, center). Discusses recent developments in both Testaments (e.g., for OT: von Rad, Zimmerli, and the program set by B. S. Childs).

13   G. E. Ladd. "Biblical Theology, History of." Pp. 498–505 and "Biblical Theology, Nature of," pp. 505–9 in $ISBE^2$, 1979.

Under "history" Ladd, a prominent evangelical, elaborates on
the era described as "victory of religion over theology," and
offers brief summaries of W. Eichrodt, L. Köhler, T. C. Vriezen,
G. E. Wright, and others. Under "nature" Ladd includes topics such as history, revelation, unity/diversity, methodology,
and goal. Helpful bibliography.

14   W. Zimmerli. "Biblische Theologie I: Altes Testament." Pp.
     426–55 in *TRZ*. Vol. 6. Berlin: Walter de Gruyter, 1980.
     An expansive article by a noted German biblical theologian.
     Reviews the history of the discipline and the attempted inte-
     gration of prophetic, historical, and Wisdom material into a
     "theology."

15   N. W. Porteous and R. E. Clements. "Old Testament Theology."
     Pp. 406–13 in *The Westminster Dictionary of Christian Theol-
     ogy*. Edited by A. Richardson and J. Bowden. Philadelphia: West-
     minster, 1983.
     Surveys the nature of the controversy surrounding the disci-
     pline, illustrates solutions primarily from Eichrodt and von
     Rad, but notes F. Baumgärtel and many others. Cf. in the same
     volume "Biblical Theology" by J. H. Houlden, pp. 69–71.

16   G. F. Hasel. "Biblical Theology Movement." Pp. 149–50 in *Evan-
     gelical Dictionary of Theology*. Edited by W. A. Elwell. Grand
     Rapids: Baker, 1984.
     Notes characteristics of the movement (e.g., alliance with neo-
     orthodoxy) and its decline. Regards it as a major attempt "to
     correct liberal theology from within itself."

17   P. D. Hanson. "Theology, Old Testament." Pp. 1057–62 in
     Harper's Bible Dictionary. Edited by P. J. Achtemeier. San Fran-
     cisco: Harper & Row, 1985.
     Treats task, starting point, issues, and the dynamic historical
     character of the discipline as represented by B. W. Anderson,
     W. Brueggemann, and P. D. Hanson. Limited bibliography.

18   J. H. Hayes. "Theology of the Old Testament." Pp. 904–8 in *Mer-
     cer Dictionary of the Bible*. Edited by Watson E. Mills. Macon,
     Ga.: Mercer University Press, 1990.
     Rehearses the history by centuries; presents six proposals for
     the future of the discipline.

19   W. Lemke. "Theology: Old Testament." Pp. 448–73 in *ABD*. Vol.
     6. Edited by D. N. Freedman. New York: Doubleday, 1992.

An unusually helpful article charting the history and issues of the discipline. Includes surveys of the works of more than a dozen OT theologians. Cf. in the same volume H. G. Reventlow's "Theology (Biblical), History of," pp. 483–505.

1.3 Theological Dictionaries and Word Books

This category includes two kinds of reference works. One set of tools discusses Hebrew words (lexemes), giving attention to their etymology and linguistic features with the aim of setting forth their theological import. The conclusions have been criticized (e.g., J. Barr, *The Semantics of Biblical Language* [Oxford: Oxford University Press, 1961]). For an evaluation of this methodology, see P. Cotterell's "Linguistics, Meaning, Semantics, and Discourse Analysis." Pp. 134–60 in *NIDOTTE*, Vol. 1 (#32).

The second set of tools discusses theology by topics keyed to English terms; some works are not limited to OT but extend their discussion to the entire Bible.

20   R. B. Girdlestone. *Synonyms of the Old Testament: Their Bearing on Christian Doctrine.* Second Edition: 1897. Reproduction of Second Edition: Grand Rapids: Eerdmans, 1948.
       More than thirty major concepts (e.g., sin, righteousness, worship/praise/preach) are treated in informative essays explaining the various nuances of Hebrew synonyms. Some remarks also on NT usage. Subject, Scripture, and Hebrew/Greek indexes. A substantive, enduring, though somewhat dated work.

21   *A Theological Wordbook of the Bible.* Edited by A. Richardson. New York: Macmillan, 1950.
       A discussion of topics of "theological interest" (e.g., Wisdom) with minimal reference to words in Hebrew and Greek. Short but clear articles by thirty-one primarily British and Protestant scholars. Useful for "English-only" readers.

22   *Vocabulary of the Bible.* Edited by J.-J. von Allmen. London: Lutterworth, 1958. Translated from the Second Edition: 1956. Original Title: *Vocabulaire Biblique.* Paris: Delachaux & Niestlé, 1954.
       A nontechnical treatment by French and Swiss Protestant scholars of 350 important biblical terms (e.g., glory). Stress is on theology rather than linguistic background.

23 *Theological Dictionary of the New Testament (TDNT).* 10 vols.
    Edited by G. Kittel and G. Friedrich. Translated and edited by
    G. W. Bromiley. Grand Rapids: Eerdmans, 1964–76.
    Original Title: *Theologisches Wörterbuch zum Neuen Testament.*
    Stuttgart: W. Kohlhammer Verlag, 1933–78.
    Full treatments of significant theological Greek words in
    alphabetical order. Frequent discussion of OT background and
    Hebrew words. Bibliography. The index volume (vol. 10) com-
    piled by R. E. Pitkin contains a three-page index of Hebrew
    words.

24 *Dictionary of Biblical Theology.* Edited by X. Léon-Dufour.
    Translated by P. J. Cahill. New York: Desclée, 1967. Second Edi-
    tion: New York: Seabury, 1973. Original Title: *Vocabulaire de
    théologie Biblique.* Paris: Les Editions du Cerf, 1962. Second Edi-
    tion: 1968.
    A classic reference work translated into numerous languages
    (e.g., German, Spanish, Italian, Croatian, Russian, Chinese,
    Japanese, Vietnamese). Intended largely for pastors. A syn-
    thetic theme approach rather than semantic analysis. Second
    edition adds forty new articles and has fuller cross-references.
    An analytic table and index are included. No bibliographies.

25 *Theological Dictionary of the Old Testament (TDOT).* Vols. 1–8
    (in process; 12 vols. projected). Edited by G. J. Botterweck,
    H. Ringgren, and H. J. Fabry. Translated by J. T. Willis, G. W.
    Bromily, and D. E. Greene. Grand Rapids: Eerdmans, 1974– . Rev.
    ed. of vols. 1 and 2 in 1977. Original Title: *Theologisches Wörter-
    buch zum Alten Testament.* Vols. 1–8. Stuttgart: W. Kohlham-
    mer, 1970–95.
    A standard work known as "OT Kittel," which lists signifi-
    cant theological Hebrew words in alphabetical order and offers
    extensive discussions regarding etymology, semantic field,
    synonyms, OT usage, and theological considerations. Articles
    include bibliography.

26 *The New International Dictionary of New Testament Theology
    (NIDNTT).* 3 vols. Edited by C. Brown. Grand Rapids: Zonder-
    van, 1975, 1976, 1978. Translated by C. Brown with additions
    and revisions. Original Title: *Theologisches Begriffslexikon zum
    Neuen Testament.* Edited by L. Coenen, E. Beyreuther, and
    H. Bietenhard. Wuppertal: Theologicher Verlag Rolf Brockhaus,
    1967, 1969, 1971.

Keyed to English words (e.g., righteousness), but the essays treat Greek terms relevant to the topic. Essays commonly identify and sometimes elaborate on the Hebrew term behind the Greek. The Hebrew terms are indexed in volume 3. Bibliographies. Recommended for those who desire a single somewhat technical theological wordbook.

27 *Theological Wordbook of the Old Testament (TWOT)*. 2 vols. Edited by R. L. Harris, G. L. Archer, and B. K. Waltke. Chicago: Moody, 1980.

A tool for the pastor that discusses significant Hebrew words in alphabetical order, while sometimes grouping related words. The forty-six contributors stand in the evangelical tradition. The 1,400 articles, usually brief, also include bibliographies. For the English-only reader, a cross-index from the "Hebrew word number" in *Strong's Concordance* is supplied.

28 *Nelson's Expository Dictionary of the Old Testament*. Edited by M. F. Unger and W. White. Nashville: Nelson, 1980.

Unsigned articles by a dozen contributors treating five hundred significant OT words arranged by their English-language equivalents. Cross-index of related terms. A useful work; helpful for those with a minimal knowledge of Hebrew.

29 *Encyclopedia of Biblical Theology: The Complete Sacramentum Verbi*. Edited by J. B. Bauer. Translated from the third enlarged and revised edition of 1967 by J. Blenkinsopp, D. J. Bourke, N. D. Smith, and W. P. van Stigt. New York: Crossroad, 1981. Original Title: *Bibeltheologisches Wörterbuch*. 2 vols. Graz: Verlag Styria, 1959. Second Edition: 1962. Third Enlarged and Revised Edition: 1967. Fourth Fully Revised Edition: 1994. Translated into several languages (e.g., *Diccionario de telogíabíblica* [Barcelona: Editorial Herder, 1967]).

Articles with bibliographies in this well-respected work are by topic (e.g., hope), noting relevant OT, ANE, and Qumran as well as NT material. Limited references to Hebrew and Greek terms. Termed "an outstanding example of the renewal in Catholic biblical scholarship." Indexes to biblical references, Greek words, and Hebrew words. Bibliography.

30 L. O. Richards. *Expository Dictionary of Bible Words*. Grand Rapids: Zondervan, 1985.

Keyed to English words, articles often include comments on Hebrew and Greek words (transliterated). Indexes to subjects,

Greek and Hebrew words, and Scripture references. Designed
for the general Bible student.

31 *Evangelical Dictionary of Biblical Theology.* Edited by W. A.
Elwell. Grand Rapids: Baker, 1996.
A compendium of key theological themes (e.g., law, priest)
prepared by more than forty contributors. While based on
Hebrew and Greek, the articles, which range over the entire
Bible, are geared toward the English reader. Very valuable. Rec-
ommended.

32 *New International Dictionary of Old Testament Theology and
Exegesis (NIDOTTE).* Edited by W. A. Van Gemeren. Vols. 1–5.
Grand Rapids: Zondervan, 1997.
Arranged by Hebrew words. Articles treat the theological
nuances of a term where appropriate and otherwise provide
exegetical information. Lexical entries, ten methodologically
oriented essays, general articles on major subjects (e.g., sacrifice), and essays on the biblical theology of each OT book make
this a highly valuable and up-to-date resource.

33 *Theological Lexicon of the Old Testament.* 3 vols. Translated by
M. E. Biddle. Peabody, Mass.: Hendrickson, 1997. Orginal Title:
Theologisches Handwoerterbunch zum Alten Testament. 2 vols.
Edited by E. Jenni and C. Westermann. Munich: Chr. Kaiser/
Zurich: Theologischer Verlag, 1971–75.

2

Serial Literature

2.1 Journals

Certain journals, as in the annotations below, are oriented largely to biblical theology. Articles on subjects of OT theology appear occasionally also in the following biblical studies journals: *CBQ, EQ, ExpTim, JSOT, OTE, SJT, TT, TynBul, ThSt, ThZ, TLZ, VT, ZAW, ZTK.*

34 *Interpretation: A Journal of Bible and Theology (Int).* Published quarterly by Union Theological Seminary, Richmond, Va., 1946– .
Devoted to communication among biblical theologians, ministers, and lay people of the church. The journal began in conjunction with the Biblical Theology Movement.

35 *Biblical Theology Bulletin (BTB).* Published quarterly, initially at the Collegio Internazionale del Gesu, Rome, Italy, with L. Sabourin, editor; incorporated at St. John's University, Jamaica, N.Y., 1971– .
The stated purpose is to "expose and discuss the present state and the progress of research in biblical theology and exegesis." Frequent articles on themes of OT theology.

36 *Horizons in Biblical Theology: An International Dialogue (HBT).* Published semiannually by Pittsburgh Theological Seminary. Initial editor: Ulrich Mauser, 1979– .
"Provides a forum for biblical interpreters who share the view that the correlation of Old and New Testament is an essen-

tial hermeneutical guide for a Christian understanding of the
Bible."

37   *Jahrbuch für Biblische Theologie (JBTh).* Published annually by
Neukirchener Verlag, 1986– .
A cadre of German editors, including N. Lohfink and W. H.
Schmidt, have linked up with Paul Hanson (Harvard), Ulrich
Mauser (Pittsburgh), and Magne Saebø to produce an annual
that is intended for biblical scholars, but also for theologians
generally as well as for pastors. Each annual takes up a differ-
ent topic related to the interdisciplinary discussion of OT and
NT (e.g., vol. 1: unity and diversity in biblical theology; vol.
4: law; vol. 9: sin and judgment).

2.2 Monograph Series

Since the task of synthesizing OT themes in an overall schema is
so demanding and the methodology so controversial, scholars and publishers chose to focus on bite-sized subjects. Beginning in the mid-
twentieth century at the time of the Biblical Theology Movement,
several publication series, representing varying viewpoints on the theological spectrum, have been inaugurated. It is generally the hope that
by exploring constitutive themes of biblical theology, help and insight
will come for the preparation of more comprehensive works.

38   Studies in Biblical Theology (SBT[1] and SBT[2])
Published by SCM of London, the series between 1950 and
1963 included thirty-seven titles, twelve of them concerned
with OT. Generally congenial to the neo-orthodox perspective. See, for example, Eichrodt (#421); Wright (#258).
In a new series, SBT,[2] begun in 1967 by the same publisher,
Studies in Biblical Theology, Second Series, fourteen of the
thirty-two titles (until 1976) dealt with OT subjects (e.g., Zimmerli [#451]).

39   Overtures to Biblical Theology (OBT)
A series initiated in 1977 with editors Walter Brueggemann
(OT) and J. R. Donahue (NT), and later expanded to include
Christopher Seitz (OT) and Sharyn Dowd (NT). Publisher:
Fortress. Annotations occur at Brueggemann (#481) and Tri-
ble (#464).

40   Studies in OT Biblical Theology (SOTBT)

This series, edited by W. A. Van Gemeren and T. Longman III, was launched in 1994 and will be published by Zondervan. Volumes focus on single theological topics, offer background and development, and show connections with the NT. See, for example, Longman (#512) and Brown (#472).

41   New Studies in Biblical Theology (NSBT)
This series, begun in 1996 by Eerdmans with D. A. Carson as editor, will address issues in biblical theology and exposit on biblical themes and thought structures of biblical books. An early examplar is R. C. Ortlund Jr. *Whoredom: God's Unfaithful Wife in Biblical Theology*, 1996.

2.3 Collected Essays

This section includes books or essays that are in part or altogether devoted to OT and/or biblical theology, but because the contents are of diverse nature, as in festschrifts, are not readily categorized. These works are cross-referenced in subsequent annotations.

42   B. W. Anderson (ed.). *The Old Testament and Christian Faith: A Theological Discussion (OTCF)*. New York: Harper & Row, 1963. Reprinted: New York: Herder & Herder, 1969.
Essays are presented by biblical scholars such as R. Bultmann, Alan Richardson, J. L. McKenzie, and Emil Brunner. Cf. C. Westermann, "The Way of Promise through the Old Testament," and B. W. Anderson, "The New Covenant and the Old." Several essays appeared in German publications and were translated.

43   C. Westermann (ed.). *Essays on Old Testament Hermeneutics (EOTH)*. Translations edited by J. L. Mays. Richmond: John Knox, 1963. Third Printing: 1966. Published in England as *Essays on Old Testament Interpretation*. London: SCM, 1963. Original Title: *Probleme alttestamentlicher Hermeneutik*. München: Chr. Kaiser Verlag, 1960.
A series of programmatic essays for the *Biblischer Kommentar* series in the early 1950s were published in *EvTh* 12 (1952), and some were later incorporated into the German book cited above. The essays treat interpretation, but some, such as "Theocracy and Soteriology" by T. C. Vriezen, and "Promise and Fulfillment" by W. Zimmerli, shade off into OT theology.

44 R. B. Laurin (ed.). *Contemporary Old Testament Theologians.* Valley Forge, Pa.: Judson/London: Marshall, Morgan & Scott, 1970. Contains summaries, analyses of structure and content, and evaluations of OT theologies: W. Eichrodt (N. K. Gottwald); G. von Rad (G. H. Davies); O. Procksch (J. N. Schofield); T. C. Vriezen (R. E. Clements); E. Jacob (R. B. Laurin); G. A. F. Knight (J. I. Durham); and P. Van Imschoot (D. A. Hubbard).

45 H. W. Wolff (ed.). *Probleme biblischer Theologie. Gerhard von Rad zum 70. Geburtstag.* Munich: Chr. Kaiser, 1971. Forty essays, mostly by German scholars. Several deal with theological themes, such as anthropology, revelation, monarchy, and salvation history.

46 W. Brueggemann and H. W. Wolff. *The Vitality of Old Testament Traditions.* Atlanta: John Knox, 1975. Two well-known OT scholars offer essays on the kerygma of the various Pentateuchal strata (J, E, D, P).

47 H. Donner, R. Hanhart, and R. Smend (eds.). *Beiträge zur Alttestamentlichen Theologie: Festschrift für Walther Zimmerli zum 70 Geburtstag.* Göttingen: Vandenhoeck und Ruprecht, 1977. Forty essays, a few in English. Among those more germane to OT theology: the essential message of the prophets (H. W. Wolff), the "good" in the OT (C. Westermann), and the theology of Micah (J. L. Mays).

48 H. Gese. *Essays on Bibical Theology.* Translated by K. Crim. Minneapolis: Augsburg, 1981. Original Title: *Zur Biblischen Theologie: Alttestamentliche Vorträge.* Munich: Chr. Kaiser Verlag, 1977. Gese, in the mode of von Rad's tradition history, traces six themes from the OT into the NT: death, the law, the atonement, passover/Lord's Supper, the Messiah, and the prologue to John's Gospel.

49 G. M. Tucker, D. L. Petersen, and R. R. Wilson (eds.). *Canon, Theology and Old Testament Interpretation: Essays in Honor of Brevard S. Childs.* Philadelphia: Fortress, 1988. Part I, "Canon and Theology," includes five essays on subjects pertinent to OT theology; for example, Barr (#105).

50 J. Reumann (ed.). *The Promise and Practice of Biblical Theology.* Minneapolis: Fortress, 1991. Five essays indicate the cutting edge of the discipline (e.g., Trible [#143]; Harrington, "The Jewishness of Jesus"). Several faculty members of Lutheran Theological Seminary, Philadelphia, note practical implications as in preaching. Valuable for its bibliographic index.

51   R. B. Zuck (ed.). *A Biblical Theology of the Old Testament.* Chicago: Moody, 1991.

With the kingdom principle (Gen. 1:26–28) as the center of biblical theology, five Dallas Theological Seminary authors, but chiefly E. H. Merrill and R. B. Chisholm Jr., describe the theology of corpora (e.g., Pentateuch, Wisdom) and individual books (e.g., Isaiah, Psalms).

52   W. Brueggemann. *Old Testament Theology: Essays on Structure, Theme, and Text.* Edited by P. D. Miller. Minneapolis: Fortress, 1992.

A reprint of essays by a prolific writer and stimulating theologian. Demonstrates with a theological flare how literary and rhetorical studies of texts (e.g., Gen. 50:15–21; 2 Sam. 21–24; Jer. 9:22–23) are tools for theological readings. Other essays deal with themes (e.g., God's presence) and assessments of suggestions for the discipline (e.g., "Futures in Old Testament Theology"). All but one of the fifteen essays have previously appeared in print.

53   R. L. Hubbard Jr., R. K. Johnston, and R. P. Meye (eds.). *Studies in Old Testament Theology.* Dallas, Tex.: Word, 1992.

The festschrift to David A. Hubbard, long-term president of Fuller Seminary, opens with three chapters on methodology, including a succinct essay on "Doing Old Testament Theology Today." The historical images of Yahweh and Yahweh's people, Israel, are traced by six scholars in six chapters with attention to the canonical ordering of Torah, Prophets, and Writings. Three more chapters indicate the contemporary relevance of these nuanced images.

54   B. C. Ollenburger, E. A. Martens, and G. F. Hasel (eds.). *The Flowering of Old Testament Theology: A Reader in Twentieth-Century Old Testament Theology, 1930–1990 (FOTT).* Sources for Biblical and Theological Study, 1. Winona Lake, Ind.: Eisenbrauns, 1992.

Excerpts from the programmatic works of twenty-one theologians, with biographical and summary introductions for each, comprise the heart of this reader. Three survey essays by the editors review (1) the history of the discipline, (2) the current landscape, and (3) future directions. Seminal essays by Eissfeldt (1926) and Eichrodt (1929) appear for the first time in English translation. An appendix presents an English translation of J. P. Gabler's 1787 oration. Useful as a class textbook and as an overview of the discipline.

55   R. Rendtorff. *Canon and Theology. Overtures to an Old Testament Theology.* OBT. Translated and edited by M. Kohl. Minneapolis: Fortress, 1993. Original Title: *Kanon und Theologie: Vorarbeiten zu einer Theologie des Alten Testaments.* Neukirchen-Vluyn: Neukirchener Verlag, 1991.

A collection of essays, most of which have been previously published, on how one does OT theology on dealing with text rather than with reconstructions; on utilizing Jewish readings; and so refusing to read the NT back into the OT. Several essays treat compositional analyses in Isaiah (3x) and Ezekiel (2x).

56   S. E. Balentine and J. W. Barton (eds.). *Language, Theology and the Bible: Essays in Honour of James Barr.* Oxford: Clarendon, 1994.

The twenty-five essays include one by J. W. Barton on J. Barr as critic and theologian, and two that bear on the theology of biblical books. See Mays (#381) and Miller (#327).

57   R. P. Knierim. *The Task of Old Testament Theology: Substance, Method, and Cases.* Grand Rapids/Cambridge: Eerdmans, 1995.

Stimulating, provocative, and probing essays by a widely recognized *alttestamentler* spanning twenty-five years. Subjects include the task of OT theology, interpretation of Gabler, revelation in the OT, hope, spirituality, land, justice, exegesis of Psalm 19, and a theology of the Book of Numbers.

58   S. J. Kraftchick, C. D. Myers Jr., and B. C. Ollenburger (eds.). *Biblical Theology: Problems and Perspectives. In Honor of J. Christiaan Beker.* Nashville: Abingdon, 1995.

Seventeen essays grouped around (1) Bible and theology in church history; (2) the problems and methods of biblical theology; (3) proposals for biblical theology (four essays by B. W. Anderson, P. D. Miller, W. Brueggemann, and K. M. O'Connor); and (4) biblical theology and theological practice.

59   H. T. C. Sun, Keith L. Eades, J. M. Robinson, and G. I. Moller (eds). *Problems in Biblical Theology: Essays in Honor of Rolf Knierim.* Grand Rapids: Eerdmans, 1997.

Twenty-five essays, several of which interact with Knierim's programmatic essays (#100, #169): R. Rentdorff, "Approaches to Old Testament Theology" (pp. 13–26); M. H. Floyd, "Cosmos and History in Zechariah's View of the Restoration (Zechariah 1:7–6:15)" (pp. 125–44); Burke O. Long, "Letting Rival Gods Be Rivals: Biblical Theology in a Postmodern Age" (pp. 222–33); E. A. Martens, "Yahweh's Compassion and Ecotheology" (pp. 234–48); W. Pannenberg, "Problems in a Theology of (Only) the Old Testament" (pp. 275–80); and C. Westermann, "Gottes Handeln und Gottes Reden in Alten Testament" (pp. 389–403).

Other essays: G. J. Brooke, "The Qumran Scrolls and Old Testament Theology" (pp. 59–75); R. E. Murphy, "Reflections on a Critical Biblical Theology" (pp. 265–74); and M. A. Sweeney, "Tanak versus Old Testament: Concerning the Foundation for a Jewish Theology of the Bible" (pp. 353–72).

3

History of the Discipline/ State of the Discipline

A form of biblical theology, often tied to dogmatics, was in vogue at the time of the Reformation. In the latter part of the eighteenth century, biblical theology was self-consciously defined as distinct from dogmatic theology in both methodology and aim. Around 1800, the discipline was shaped largely by concerns arising out of rational philosophy. In a conservative reaction, the category of history, specifically Heilsgeschichte, became constitutive of biblical theological writings. A shift to preoccupation with the history of Israelite religion eclipsed OT theology for almost fifty years (ca. 1875–1925). Following World War I, fresh voices called for a return to biblical theology; a significant exemplar was W. Eichrodt, whose work on OT theology was published in 1933. The twentieth century has witnessed an impressive outpouring of books on the subject.

Succinct historical accounts are found in dictionary articles, section 1.2 (e.g., Lemke [#19] and Reventlow [#19]), and as chapters in monographs such as Hasel (#95, pp. 10–27) and Smith (#83, pp. 21–71).

60   G. F. Oehler. *Prolegomena zur Theologie des Alten Testaments.* Stuttgart: S. G. Liesching, 1845.
      "The first systematic study of the history and methodology of OT theology" (Hasel [#80], p. 136).

61   J. D. Smart. "The Death and Rebirth of Old Testament Theology." *JR* 23 (1943): 1–11, 125–36.

Offers reason for the "death" of OT theology (e.g., the shift in general ethos away from theology to history) in the latter part of the nineteenth century and reasons for its revival in the early twentieth century. A fine orientation article.

62 N. W. Porteous. "Old Testament Theology." Pp. 311–44 in *The Old Testament and Modern Study*. Edited by H. H. Rowley. Oxford: Clarendon, 1951. Reprinted: Oxford: University Press, 1956.

Reviews in some detail the views of A. B. Davidson, O. Eissfeldt, and W. Eichrodt; lists works that appeared in the 1930s and 1940s and pursues the question of the "proper nature of an Old Testament theology."

63 H. F. Hahn. "The Theological Approach to the Old Testament." Pp. 226–49 in *Old Testament in Modern Research*. Philadelphia: Muhlenberg, 1954. Expanded Edition: Philadelphia: Fortress, 1966.

Narrates the development in OT theology for the first half of the twentieth century by referencing German scholars and neo-orthodox scholars in England and America.

64 E. J. Young. *The Study of Old Testament Theology Today.* London: James Clarke, 1958.

Four lectures given at the London Bible College by a professor at Westminster Theological Seminary on OT theology: its history, nature, content, and influence.

65 N. W. Porteous. "The Present State of Old Testament Theology." *ExpTim* 75 (1963): 70–74. Cf. his "The Theology of the Old Testament." Pp. 151–59 in *Peake's Commentary on the Bible*. Edited by M. Black and H. H. Rowley. London: Thomas Nelson & Sons, 1963.

Largely a response to J. Barr's challenge to biblical theologians made in his books *The Semantics of Biblical Language* (1961) and *Biblical Words for Time* (1962). Also comments on constructing a theology, and notes the works of E. Jacob, W. Eichrodt, and G. von Rad. For contours of an OT theology, see Porteous's article in *Peake's* commentary.

66 B. S. Childs. *Biblical Theology in Crisis*. Philadelphia: Westminster, 1970.

Treats the development of OT theology in America, analyzes the so-called Biblical Theology Movement, and proposes the canon as the context for biblical theology.

67 W. H. Schmidt. "Theologie des Alten Testaments 'vor und nach von Rad.'" *Verkündigung und Forschung* 17 (1972): 1–25.
Sketches broadly the theological directions taken by theologians from J. P. Gabler on. Focuses more extensively on W. Eichrodt and his successors, and on H. Gese, who followed von Rad. Concludes with ten thesis statements about OT theology. For a more detailed history, cf. Kraus (#203).

68 J. Barr. "Trends and Prospects in Biblical Theology." *JTS* 25 (1974): 265–82.
Surveys recent literature and discusses salient problems, such as center, canon, history of religion approach, and the relationship between the OT and Jewish religion.

69 R. E. Clements. *One Hundred Years of Old Testament Interpretation*. Philadelphia: Westminster, 1976.
In a chapter on OT theology, Clements summarizes developments from H. Schultz (1869) to G. von Rad (1960).

70 M. E. Tate. "Old Testament Theology: The Current Situation." *RevExp* 74.3 (1977): 279–300.
A helpful article on methodological approaches taken by OT theologians; comments also on the nature of the discipline. Amply documented.

71 G. F. Hasel. "The Future of Biblical Theology." Pp. 179–94 in *Perspectives on Evangelical Theology*. Edited by S. N. Gundry and K. S. Kantzer. Grand Rapids: Baker, 1979.
Advances theses on the place, method, content, task, structure (proposes a multiplex approach), and challenge of biblical theology. Amply footnoted.

72 J. D. Smart. *The Past, Present, and Future of Biblical Theology*. Philadelphia: Westminster, 1979.
A series of semi-popular lectures. Interacts with B. S. Childs (#66); discusses emphases in interpretation, such as historicism and neo-orthodoxy. Urges that the biblical texts be allowed to make their theological witness (p. 196). Touches on problems concerning revelation, history, and systematic theology.

73 W. Brueggemann. "A Convergence in Recent Old Testament Theologies." *JSOT* 18 (1980): 2–18. Reprinted in Brueggemann (#52, pp. 95–110).
Reviews the works of C. Westermann, S. Terrien, and P. Hanson and exposits the dialectic in each.

74 G. F. Hasel. "A Decade of Old Testament Theology: Retrospect and Prospect." *ZAW* 93.2 (1981): 165–83.

Heavily footnoted (e.g., former overviews), the review covers the decade of 1969–78 via approaches such as the historical-genetic, cross-section, topical/thematic, and diachronic. Concludes with proposals for a multiplex approach.

75 W. Brueggemann. "Futures in Old Testament Theology." *HBT* 6 (1984): 1–11. Reprinted in Brueggemann (#52, pp. 111–17).

A fresh shape may be emerging: the double trajectory pattern à la P. D. Hanson and J. A. Sanders (e.g., visionary/pragmatic, prophetic/constitutive). One might cease asking about center, asking instead about boundaries.

76 J. H. Hayes and F. C. Prussner. *Old Testament Theology: Its History and Development.* Atlanta: John Knox, 1985.

An expansion, revision, and update by Hayes of Prussner's doctoral dissertation, *Methodology in Old Testament Theology*, part one, 1952. Attention is given to the theological milieu for each period beginning with the Reformation. Half the book treats the pre–1920 period. Helpful summaries of books by biblical theologians. A standard work.

77 S. Terrien. "Biblical Theology: The Old Testament (1970–1984): A Decade and a Half of Spectacular Growth." *BTB* 15.4 (1985): 127–35.

A sequel to J. Harvey's article, "The New Diachronic Biblical Theology of the Old Testament, 1960–1970." *BTB* 1 (1971): 5–29. Terrien sketches the state of the discipline through brief, often evaluative comments on the published works of those in the field.

78 B. Janowski. "Literatur zur biblischen Theologie 1982–1985." *JBTh* 1 (1986): 210–44.

Lists more than five hundred books and essays, mostly in German, on the current debate in the discipline. Valuable for listings on topics such as covenant, justice and righteousness, law and gospel, kingdom of God, life and death.

79 H. G. Reventlow. "Zur Theologie des Alten Testaments." *ThR* 52.3 (1987): 221–67.

A wide-ranging bibliographic essay, a sequel to E. Wurthwein's essay (*ThR* 36 [1971]: 185–208). Summaries of forty books, half of them in English, are given.

80   G. F. Hasel. "Old Testament Theology from 1978–1987." *AUSS* 26.2 (1988): 133–57.
Reviews OT theologies of the period with an emphasis on history and development, methodology and structures, issues of "center" and "descriptive or normative."

81   R. Smend. *Deutsche Alttestamentler in drei Jahrhunderten: mit 18 Abbildungen.* Göttingen: Vandenhoeck und Ruprecht, 1989.
Of the eighteen scholars noted, biographical essays are devoted to four OT theologians: K. Marti, B. Stade, G. von Rad, and W. Zimmerli.

82   J. Reumann. "Introduction: Whither Biblical Theology?" Pp. 1–31 in *The Promise and Practice of Biblical Theology* (#50).
A bibliographical essay sorting out possible approaches to the discipline. Ten pages of bibliography helpfully classified.

83   R. L. Smith. *Old Testament Theology: Its History, Method, and Message.* Nashville: Broadman & Holman, 1993.
An entry-level but useful introduction to OT theology. The story of the discipline is concise and well told (pp. 21–71); the discussion on methods is cursory. The bulk of the book is largely a gathering of quotes by notable OT theologians collated according to theme (e.g., the knowledge of God, sin and redemption, worship, death and beyond). Helpful for teachers in buttressing lectures.

84   R. Gnuse. "New Directions in Biblical Theology." *JAAR* 62 (1994): 893–918.
A review essay of developments since World War II, noting especially the demise of Heilsgeschichte and the emergence of new paradigms that grapple with the social-historical and religious origins of Israel. A theological idiom that resonates with these trends is process thought.

85   G. F. Hasel. "The Nature of Biblical Theology: Recent Trends and Issues." *AUSS* 32.3 (1994): 203–15.
The first of three essays by a well-known observer of the discipline. Reviews major publications since 1990, and describes key elements of the Biblical Theology Movement and what followed. Cf. "Recent Models of Biblical Theology: Three Major Perspectives," *AUSS* 33.1–2 (1995): 55–75. The three perspectives are those of J. J. Collins (critical biblical theology), B. S. Childs (canonical approach), and H. Hübner (restricted biblical theology). Cf. also "Proposal

for a Canonical Biblical Theology." *AUSS* 34.1 (1996): 23–33. Hasel offers seven theses. The approach is to be theological-historical, and the structure to encompass the multiform biblical materials. The third essay was published after Hasel's death.

86 B. S. Childs. "Old Testament Theology." Pp. 293–301 in *Old Testament Interpretation: Past, Present, and Future. Essays in Honor of Gene M. Tucker.* Edited by J. L. Mays, D. L. Petersen, and K. H. Richards. Nashville: Abingdon, 1995.

Chiefly outlines trends (e.g., insights from social sciences, narrative theology, holistic reading, feminist and liberation theologies) and future directions for the discipline.

87 S. J. Kraftchick. "Facing Janus: Reviewing the Biblical Theology Movement." Pp. 54–77 in *Biblical Theology: Problems and Perspectives* (#58).

The concerns of the Biblical Theological Movement are illustrated via H. H. Rowley and Paul Minear. Critique is offered via J. Barr and L. Gilkey, and lessons are drawn.

88 D. Penchansky. *The Politics of Biblical Theology: A Postmodern Reading.* Macon, Ga.: Mercer University Press, 1995.

Focuses on forces that shape the interpretation process. Analyzes the "political core" of the Biblical Theology Movement as represented by Thorlief Bowman and G. Ernest Wright, but also the subjective political considerations of its detractors, James Barr and Langdon Gilkey.

89 H. G. Reventlow. "Theologie und Hermeneutik des Alten Testaments." *ThR* 61.1–2 (1996): 48–102, 123–76.

A bibliographical essay by a highly respected monitor of the discipline. Summarizes and briefly assesses literature appearing largely in German but also in English since 1987 according to categories such as method, OT theology, panbiblical theologies, and Christian–Jewish dialogue. Cf. his "Zur Theologie des Alten Testaments." *ThR* 52.3 (1987): 221–67. A helpful supplement to Hasel's (#95).

90 E. A. Martens. "The Flowering and Foundering of Old Testament Theology." Vol. 1. Pp. 172–84 in *NIDOTTE* (#32).

Discusses the topic under the headings of divergent objectives, shifting orientations (e.g., the literary/linguistic angle of vision), and ambiguity about method.

91   R. Rendtorff. "Recent German Old Testament Theologies." *JR*
        76 (1996): 328–37.
        Reviews works by H. D. Preuss (#308), A. H. J. Gunneweg
        (#304), O. Kaiser (#305), and J. Schreiner (#309) and also notes
        the renewed discussion, prompted by Rainer Albertz, about
        Old Testament theology versus the history of Israelite reli-
        gion (#128).

4

Issues in the Discipline

The fortunes of this discipline have been unpredictable, partly because debate continues on a series of issues. Consensus on method, perspective, and even points of departure is elusive.

A basic issue continues to be the clarification of task, an issue muddied by differences of opinion on how the discipline relates to other biblical disciplines. Moreover, practitioners as well as theorists are not united on the method appropriate to the discipline. G. F. Hasel has followed the trends most assiduously, as the revised editions of his *Old Testament Theology: Basic Issues in the Current Debate* testify.

Cultural agenda and interests impinge on the discipline. Earlier, the rubric of history was dominant as a factor in the interpretative process. A strong emphasis on the historical dimension, however, leaves unsettled the matter of where wisdom is to be placed, not to mention whether other approaches such as the sociological or the literary might be more productive. Some have thought it desirable to structure a theology around a center; others dispute whether such an enterprise is legitimate.

The attempt to categorize bibliographical sources is admittedly arbitrary since discussions on history and method, for example, may also include observations about task.

4.1 The Task of Old Testament Theology

The definition of the discipline and the task of OT theology are related topics that have engaged scholars. Is it the task of OT theology to offer a summary of the OT world of faith and witness? Is the enterprise concerned with textual matters, or is a theology derived from events? Can one distinguish meaningfully about what the text meant and what it means? Is the outcome to be a descriptive statement so that others may build on it and offer normative statements? Is God the sole object of the discipline, or is it statements about God, or is the horizon of investigation to include things religious generally?

In addition to sources noted here, many of the dictionary articles in §1.2 (note esp. Stendahl [#11]) raise the questions and show what answers have been supplied.

92   E. J. Young. "What Is Old Testament Biblical Theology?" *EQ* 31 (1959): 136–42.

Defines the subject as "the study of God in His progressive self-revelation in history." Young has reservations about the Biblical Theology Movement.

93   R. C. Dentan. *Preface to Old Testament Theology.* New Haven, Conn.: Yale University Press/London: Oxford University Press, 1950. Revised Edition: New York: Seabury, 1963.

Supplies the background of the discipline (pp. 15–83); then takes up aspects: nature, function, scope, and method.

94   R. de Vaux. "Is It Possible to Write a 'Theology of the Old Testament'?" Pp. 49–62 in his *The Bible and the Ancient Near East.* Translated by Damian McHugh. Garden City, N.Y.: Doubleday, 1971.

Critiques von Rad and asserts that the foundation of faith is the history as set forth in the biblical narratives.

95   G. F. Hasel. *Old Testament Theology: Basic Issues in the Current Debate.* Grand Rapids: Eerdmans, 1972. Revised Editions: 1975, 1982, 1991.

A standard book by an astute observer on the issues of the discipline: methodology, "center," history and faith, and the relationship of the Testaments. Sketches the history of OT theology (pp. 10–27). Helpful for the general reader as an overview and for the specialist for its bibliography and footnotes.

96   W. J. Harrington. *The Path of Biblical Theology.* Dublin: Gill and Macmillan, 1973.

A survey of OT theologies (primarily Eichrodt, Vriezen, Jacob, and von Rad), including contributions of Roman Catholic scholars (pp. 1–113). Methods (e.g., OT and the Christian) are addressed for the OT (pp. 349–62), for the NT, and for biblical theology. Recommended for an overall orientation.

97   J. Goldingay. "The Study of Old Testament Theology: Its Aims
      and Purpose." *TynBul* 26 (1975): 34–52.
         Discusses the question of whether OT theology is descriptive
      or normative, the relationship between OT theology and NT
      theology, and the function of the discipline (namely, to aid in
      the exposition of Scripture).

98   H. G. Reventlow. "Basic Problems in Old Testament Theology."
      JSOT 11 (1979): 2–22.
         Discusses challenges to the centrality of history and the prob-
      lem of center, and offers an outline of themes (e.g., creation,
      Wisdom).

99   J. W. Barton. "Old Testament Theology." Pp. 90–112 in *Begin-
      ning Old Testament Study*. Edited by. J. Rogerson. Philadelphia:
      Westminster, 1982.
         An entry-level article making the case for OT theology, with
      a more extended comment on the works of Eichrodt and von
      Rad.

100   R. P. Knierim. "The Task of Old Testament Theology." *HBT* 6.1
      (1984): 25–57. Reprinted together with responses in *The Task of
      Old Testament Theology* (#57, pp. 1–56). Cf. additional essays of
      interaction in Knierim's FS (#59).
         Proposes that OT theology address the plurality of theologies
      within the OT from the "ultimate vantage point," which
      Knierim regards as intrinsic to the OT itself: "the universal
      dominion of Yahweh in justice and righteousness" (p. 43).
      Responses to Knierim by W. Harrelson (pp. 59–64), R. E. Mur-
      phy (pp. 65–71), and W. Sibley Towner (pp. 73–80) appear in
      the same issue.

101   B. C. Ollenburger. "Biblical Theology: Situating the Discipline."
      Pp. 37–62 in *Understanding the Word of God: Essays in Honor
      of Bernhard W. Anderson*. Edited by J. T. Butler, E. W. Conrad,
      and B. C. Ollenburger. Sheffield: JSOT, 1985.
         Gabler's views are analyzed. Ollenburger holds that the dis-
      cipline currently is too much concerned with the task of sys-
      tematic elaborations, rather than with the concrete life of the
      community of faith. Cf. P. D. Hanson, "The Responsibility of
      Biblical Theology to the Community of Faith," *TT* (1980):
      39–50.

102   H. G. Reventlow. *Problems of Old Testament Theology in the
      Twentieth Century*. Translated by John Bowden. Philadelphia:

Fortress, 1985/London: SCM, 1986. Original Title: *Hauptprobleme der Alttestamentlichen Theologie im 20. Jahrhundert.* Erträge der Forschung, 173. Darmstadt: Wissenschaftliche Buchgesellschaft, 1982.

A bibliographic essay that discusses early beginnings of the discipline plus problems of a systematic account; history (and faith); center; and the world horizon of creation, myth, and Wisdom. An important source book for orientation to OT theology. Cf. the sequel, *Problems of Biblical Theology* (#213).

103 P. Addinall. "What Is Meant by a Theology of the Old Testament?" *ExpTim* 97.11 (1986): 332–36.

The function of an OT theology is to make the implicit metaphysics of the OT explicit; the process is illustrated by attention to creation and theodicy.

104 R. N. Whybray. "OT Theology—A Non-existent Beast?" Pp. 168–80 in *Scripture: Meaning and Method. Essays Presented to Anthony Tyrell Hanson for His Seventieth Birthday.* Edited by B. P. Thompson. Pickering, North Yorkshire: Hull University Press, 1987.

Questions the propriety of attempting a "theology" of the OT. Analyzes other ways of studying the OT (e.g., the historical).

105 J. Barr. "The Theological Case against Biblical Theology." Pp. 3–19 in *Canon, Theology, and Old Testament Interpretation: Essays in Honor of Brevard S. Childs.* Edited by G. M. Tucker, D. L. Petersen, and R. R. Wilson. Philadelphia: Fortress, 1988.

Cites theological reasons for the late-twentieth-century crisis in the discipline: God, not the Bible, should be the horizon shaping the study; methodologically OT theology has been unable to handle questions of current importance and has evaded the real problems of the modern world.

106 J. Høgenhaven. *Problems and Prospects of OT Theology.* The Biblical Seminar. Sheffield: JSOT, 1988.

Treats selected problems in the light of a historical survey beginning with 1920 (pp. 13–27): for example, method (Procksch, von Rad, Baumgärtel, Hesse), center, and relationship between the Testaments (pp. 44–68). With a focus on the canon rather than history, Høgenhaven proposes that a "summarizing description" be structured around the principal literary categories, with a lead position given to Wisdom, followed by Psalms, narrative literature, Law, and Prophets.

107 R. Rendtorff. "Must 'Biblical Theology' Be Christian Theology?"
Bible Review 4.3 (1988): 40–43.
    Despite views (listed and described) that the OT be consid-
    ered in relation to the NT, the theology of the Hebrew Bible
    should be examined independently of later religious develop-
    ments, whether Christian or Jewish.

108 H. Lempke. "Is Old Testament Theology a Christian Discipline?"
HBT 11 (1989): 59–71.
    Addresses the definition of OT theology and concludes that
    there is nothing inherent in the discipline that it should be an
    exclusively Christian theological enterprise.

109 J. J. Collins. "Is a Critical Biblical Theology Possible?" Pp. 1–17
in *The Hebrew Bible and Its Interpreters.* Edited by W. H. Propp,
B. Halpern, and D. N. Freedman. Biblical and Judaic Studies from
the University of California–San Diego. Vol. 1. Winona Lake,
Ind.: Eisenbrauns, 1990.
    "Historical criticism . . . is not compatible with a confessional
    theology. . . . It is, however, quite compatible with theology,
    understood as an open-ended and critical inquiry into the mean-
    ing and function of God-language" (p. 14).

110 R. Bornemann. "Toward a Biblical Theology." Pp. 117–28 in *The
Promise and Practice of Biblical Theology* (#50).
    Advocates that both the task and the structure of the disci-
    pline be formulated around the *religious* question: How should
    we live in our world with our neighbor in relationship to God?

111 A. G. Auld. "Can a Biblical Theology Also Be Academic or Ecumenical?" Pp. 13–27 in *Text as Pretext.* Edited by R. P. Carroll.
JSOTSup 138. Sheffield: JSOT, 1992.
    Focuses on four Jewish scholars: Jon Levenson, Moshe Goshen-
    Gottstein, Matitiahu Tsevat, and Michael Fishbane, and their
    respondents, Bernhard Anderson and Rolf Rendtorff.

112 R. L. Hubbard Jr. "Doing Old Testament Theology Today." Pp.
31–46 in *Studies in Old Testament Theology* (#53). Cf. R. E. Murphy, "Reflections on a Critical Biblical Theology" (#59).
    The problems of unity, task definition, and OT/NT relation-
    ships are briefly noted. Assumptions relating to "task" are
    elaborated, among which is the conviction that though the
    structure of an OT theology derives from the OT, the canon-
    ical context is the entire Bible.

113 R. W. L. Moberly. "The Nature of Christian Biblical Theology."
Pp. 141–57 in *From Eden to Golgatha: Essays in Biblical Theology.* South Florida Studies in the History of Judaism. Atlanta, Ga.: Scholars, 1992.
> Holds that the task of biblical theologians should be to bring Scripture to bear on Christian spirituality through an orientation to canon rather than history.

114 J. Barr. *Biblical Faith and Natural Theology: The Gifford Lectures for 1991 Delivered in the University of Edinburgh.* Oxford: Clarendon, 1993.
> A final chapter treats natural theology and the future of biblical theology.

115 P. Pokorny. "The Problem of Biblical Theology." *HBT* 15 (1993): 83–94.
> Brief discussion with helpful footnotes on three problems: revelation and history, revelation and theology (the problem of hermeneutics), and revelation and the Bible (problem of OT and NT).

4.2 Biblical Theology and Other Disciplines

Earlier, at the time of J. P. Gabler, the issue was how to define biblical theology over against dogmatic theology. Following the dearth of biblical theology in the latter part of the nineteenth century, the discussion focused sharply on the distinction between biblical theology and the history of religion (cf. Eissfeldt [#117] and Eichrodt [#118]). More recently, the earlier agenda about the connection of biblical theology with systematic theology and also with the history of religion has come again to the fore, but so have questions about connections with the disciplines of philosophy and hermeneutics.

116 J. P. Gabler. "On the Proper Distinction between Biblical and Dogmatic Theology and the Specific Objectives of Each." Translated by John Sandys-Wunsch and Laurence Eldredge. *SJT* 33 (1980): 133–44. Reprinted in *FOTT*, pp. 492–502. Original Title: "De justo discrimine theologiae et dogmaticae regundisque recte utriusque finibus." *Kleinere Theologische Schriften.* Edited by Gabler's sons. Vol. 2. Ulm, 1831, pp. 179–98. A German translation appears on pp. 273–84 in O. Merk. *Biblische Theologie des neuen Testaments in ihrer Anfangzeit.* Marburg: Elwert, 1972. A partial English translation is found in W. G. Kuemmel. *The*

New Testament: The History of the Investigation of Its Problems. London: SCM, 1973, pp. 98–100.

A lecture, often said to inaugurate the discipline, given on March 30, 1787, at the University of Altdorf, Germany. Biblical theology treats biblical ideas in their historical setting (and, therefore, "true") and offers a philosophically informed explanation of them as to which are abidingly valid ("pure"). The timeless truths are elaborated in dogmatic theology. In Cf. a recent analysis of the lecture (#129), pp. 495–556.

117   O. Eissfeldt. "The History of Israelite-Jewish Religion and Old Testament Theology." Translated by B. C. Ollenburger. Pp. 20–29 in *FOTT* (1992). Original Title: "Israelitisch-jüdische Religionsgeschichte und Alttestamentliche Theologie." *ZAW* 44 (1926): 1–12.

A classic essay that distinguishes between active knowing (history of religion) and passive believing (OT theology), and holds that the science of historical criticism is not applicable to the latter (cf. Eichrodt [#118]).

118   W. Eichrodt. "Does Old Testament Theology Still have Independent Significance within Old Testament Scholarship?" Translated by B. C. Ollenburger. Pp. 30–39 in *FOTT* (1992). Original Title: "Hat die Alttestamentliche Theologie noch selbständige Bedeutung innerhalb der Alttestamentlichen Wissenschaft?" *ZAW* 47 (1929): 83–91.

A classic essay in which, against Eissfeldt (#117), Eichrodt holds that OT theology is a legitimate scientific discipline in that historical investigation can uncover the essence of a religion.

119   W. A. Irwin. "The Reviving Theology of the Old Testament." *JR* 25 (1945): 235–46.

Takes issue with J. D. Smart (#61). "These, then, are the differences of the historical and theological treatments of Israel's religion: in arrangement and selection of material and in mood, the latter of which wears very thin."

120   C. R. North. "Old Testament Theology and the History of Hebrew Religion." *SJT* 2 (1949): 113–126, esp. pp. 122–23.

The disciplines differ in form and function, but to posit a disjunction is wrong. Holds that God/Yahweh is the unifying center of the OT.

121 E. G. Kraeling. "The Old Testament in Systematic Theology since Ritschl" and "Systematic Theology and the Old Testament after 1918." Pp. 98–125 and 164–77 in *The Old Testament since the Reformation.* New York: Harper & Brothers, 1955. Reprinted: New York: Schocken, 1969 (see #196).

   A sweeping sketch from a preoccupation with the "historical" to the emphasis in Karl Barth on the transcendent. In between, the concerns of biblical theology occasionally surface.

122 J. Blenkinsopp. *A Sketchbook of Biblical Theology.* New York: Herder & Herder/London: Burns & Oates, 1968.

   Written at the popular level (minimum footnotes) for Roman Catholics as an explanation of the difference between biblical and systematic theology. A series of essays, not particularly interrelated and most previously published, illustrates the biblical theology approach.

123 R. B. Gaffin Jr. "Systematic Theology and Biblical Theology." *WTJ* 38 (1976): 281–99.

   Views the question from the Reformed tradition, notes the positions of such theologians as G. Vos and John Murray on the subject, and outlines the impetus of this direction (e.g., "biblical theology is regulative of exegesis").

124 G. F. Hasel. "The Relationship between Biblical Theology and Systematic Theology." *TrinJ* 5.2 (1984): 113–27.

   Gives a brief review of history, discusses the meant/means tension à la D. H. Kelsey, and urges a biblical theology that includes both Testaments.

125 K. Jeppsen. "The Study of the Israelite Religion and Old Testament: Where Do We Stand and Where Should We Go?" *SJOT* 3.2 (1989): 140–45.

   Holds that critical-historical research is necessary for OT theology. Against B. S. Childs, but in support of J. Barr, advocates attention to the growth of tradition. A sequel article by P. Dirksen addresses what OT theology is and should be: "Israelite Religion and Old Testament Theology," *SJOT* 4.2 (1990): 96–100.

126 G. M. Tucker. "Old Testament Theology and Israelite Religion: Problems and Possibilities." *Colloquium* 22.2 (1990): 1–11.

   A seasoned scholar reviews and assesses customary distinctions between the two topics. He notes two themes from OT theology (God, history, and the world; and the human situation), and theoretical modes other than history for studying Israelite religion (e.g., time, space, gesture, and sound).

127 B. C. Ollenburger (ed.). *So Wide a Sea: Essays on Biblical and Systematic Theology*. IMS Text Reader, 4. Elkhart, Ind.: Institute of Mennonite Studies, 1991.

Seven Mennonite scholars (e.g., A. J. Reimer, G. D. Kaufman, M. Schertz, H. J. Loewen, E. A. Martens) explore the distinctions and relations between the two disciplines along theoretical lines, but also via a case study on atonement (T. Finger). The discussion tilts toward greater integration of the two disciplines.

128 R. Albertz. *A History of Israelite Religion in the Old Testament Period*. Old Testament Library. 2 vols. Translated by John Bowden. Louisville: Westminster and John Knox/London: SCM, 1994. Original Title: *Religionsgeschichte Israels in alttestamentlicher Zeit*. Göttingen: Vandenhoeck und Ruprecht, 1992.

In an opening section Albertz discusses the relationship of the history of religion to OT theology, concluding that the differences between the two are irreconcilable. He presents the case for the history of religion. Cf. his lead article in *JBTh* 10 (1995), an issue devoted to a discussion of the history of religion and biblical theology. Cf. also pp. 177–87 in the same issue, an essay more positive toward OT theology, "Hat die theologie des Alten Testaments doch noch eine Chance?"

129 R. P. Knierim. "On Gabler." Pp. 495–556 in *The Task of Old Testament Theology* (#57).

An in-depth analysis of Gabler's lecture with attention to the major issues raised (e.g., the relation of theology and religion, biblical theology, and systematic theology). An extended review of other analyses and an excursus on S. F. N. Morus, whose philosophical categories about universal notions Gabler adopted, are most helpful.

4.3 Method of Old Testament Theology

Once it was clear that biblical theology was committed to working with biblical categories, there still remained questions of method. The debate was focused with the appearance of two magisterial works, one by Walther Eichrodt (#266) and one by G. von Rad (#268). Eichrodt favored an approach that utilized *systematic* categories; von Rad advocated a *history of traditions* approach. Eichrodt described his method as a cross-cut method. G. von Rad's method was diachronic. Subsequently, some have opted for a confessional method (e.g., Vriezen); others for a dialectical method (e.g., Westermann, Terrien). G. E. Wright followed a method attentive to events; Brevard Childs' method was text-oriented.

The following articles treat mostly the methodological dimensions, but many of the entries under "Task" (§4.1) and even "History" (§3) also discuss method. For an extended discussion on method, cf. Reventlow (#102) and Hasel (#95).

130   W. Eichrodt. "Excursus: The Problem of Old Testament Theology." Pp. 512–20 in *Theology of the Old Testament* (#266).
      Responds to von Rad and sets out his own position on how to deal with history, a theological center, and typology as a way of relating the two Testaments. Cf. G. von Rad's "Postscript," pp. 410–27 in *Old Testament Theology* (#268); von Rad ranges over several topics, including historical interpretation and tradition.

131   R. E. Clements. "The Problem of Old Testament Theology." *London Quarterly and Holborn Review* 34 (1965): 11–17.
      Addresses the problem of methodology and the need to find a suitable arrangement by means of which the contents of the OT can be presented theologically (p. 11). Compares Eichrodt and von Rad, and comments on the issue of history.

132   W. G. Nesbit. *A Study of Methodologies in Contemporary Old Testament Biblical Theologies.* Ann Arbor, Mich.: University Microfilms, 1970.
      A brief reference to the work is made in *OTE* 3.2 (1990): 157.

133   D. G. Spriggs. *Two Old Testament Theologies: A Comparative Evaluation of Eichrodt and von Rad to Our Understanding of the Nature of Old Testament Theology.* London: SCM, 1974.
      Summarizes what Eichrodt intends with covenant, the function of Heilsgeschichte in von Rad, and essentially compares their methods and stances on history, the way in which each relates to the NT, and the way in which the unity of the OT as well as revelation is expressed in each. Spriggs often favors Eichrodt, but in the end tilts in von Rad's direction.

134   H. Gese. "Tradition and Biblical Theology." Pp. 301–26 in *Tradition and Theology in the Old Testament.* Edited by D. A. Knight. Philadelphia: Fortress, 1977.

Urges the importance of tradition history for biblical theology with respect to the text as a whole, the canon (especially the relationships of the Testaments), and revelation history.

135 W. E. Ward. "Towards a Biblical Theology." *RevExp* 74.3 (1977): 371–87.

Comments on the crisis (à la Childs [#66]) and Gabler's seminal lecture. Analyzes reasons for the renewal of the discipline and proposes guidelines (e.g., method to be historical exegesis).

136 W. Brueggemann. "A Convergence in Recent Old Testament Theologies." *JSOT* 18 (1980): 2–18. Reprinted in *Old Testament Theology: Essays on Structure, Theme, and Text* (#52).

Summarizes three books—all with a dialectic approach—which move beyond the options posed by Eichrodt and von Rad: Westermann (blessing/deliverance [#289]), Terrien (ethical/aesthetic [#282]), and Hanson (visionary/pragmatic, *Dynamic of Transcendence* [Philadelphia: Fortress, 1978]).

137 S. E. McEvenue. "The Old Testament: Scripture or Theology?" *Int* 35 (1981): 229–42. Reprinted in *Ex Auditu* 1 (1985): 115–24.

Identifies deficiencies in B. S. Childs' canonical approach; proposes solutions along the lines of B. Lonergan's *Method in Theology*.

138 E. Smick. "Old Testament Theology: The Historico-genetic Method." *JETS* 26 (1983): 145–55.

Reviews and appraises approaches by W. Brueggemann, B. S. Childs, and P. Hanson. "[T]he biblical theologian must have a method that will enhance the authority that the Bible claims for itself rather than undermine that authority." That method is a historico-doctrinal one that stresses the progressive nature of OT theology.

139 W. Brueggemann. "Old Testament Theology as a Particular Conversation: Adjudication of Israel's Sociotheological Alternatives." *Theology Digest* 32 (1985): 303–25. Reprinted: Pp. 119–49 in *Old Testament Theology: Essays on Structure, Theme, and Text* (#52).

Further explores organizing OT in a bipolar way (cf. Shape [#140]). Urges a sociotheological alertness, given the polarities of transformation and conservation.

140 W. Brueggemann. "A Shape for Old Testament Theology, I: Structure Legitimation." *CBQ* 47 (1985): 28–46; "A Shape for Old Testament Theology, II: Embrace of Pain." *CBQ* 47 (1985): 395–415.

Reprinted: Pp. 1–21, 22–44 in *Old Testament Theology: Essays on Structure, Theme, and Text* (#52). Excerpts, primarily from the second essay, appear in *FOTT,* pp. 409–26.

An OT theology must be bipolar, incorporating both the sanctions of common theology that appeal to order with God as the enforcer, and God's "transformation" deriving from dysfunction and entailing pain.

141 G. W. Coats. "Theology of the Hebrew Bible." Pp. 239–62 in *The Hebrew Bible and Its Modern Interpreters.* Edited by D. A. Knight and G. M. Tucker. Chico: Scholars/ Philadelphia: Fortress, 1985.

The focal issue of method is treated around key words in the discipline and is illustrated from practitioners: descriptive method (Stendahl), kerygmatic (e.g., Eichrodt, Zimmerli, von Rad), canon (Childs), and moral theology (B. C. Birch).

142 G. F. Hasel. "Major Recent Issues in Old Testament Theology 1978–1983." *JSOT* 31 (1985): 31–53.

Addresses problems related to methodology, the question of history, the matter of center, and issues in the canonical approach—all in the light of recent theologies.

143 P. Trible. "Five Loaves and Two Fishes: Feminist Hermeneutics and Biblical Theology." *Theological Studies* 50 (1989): 279–95. Excerpt in *FOTT,* pp. 448–64. For a later version, see pp. 51–70 in *The Promise and Practice of Biblical Theology* (#50).

One of the early and still relatively few probes into biblical theology from the feminist perspective. Following a brief sketch of the discipline, Trible offers overtures entailing a particular kind of exegesis and contours, including grounding in creation, wrestling with authority, and folk religion.

144 A. W. Walker-Jones. "The Role of Theological Imagination in Biblical Theology." *HBT* 11.1 (1989): 73–97.

Compares the methodologies of J. P. Gabler, W. Eichrodt, and G. von Rad. Concludes that theologians are not only historians, but "make an imaginative, synoptic theological judgment about the mode of God's presence in both Israel and the church that allows them to write a biblical theology" (pp. 92f.).

145 W. J. Wessels. "The Validity of Old Testament Theology: Eichrodt, a Forerunner of the Modern Era." *OTE* 3.2 (1990): 147–57.

In a generalized, somewhat critical fashion, Wessels apprises Eichrodt's presuppositions and truth-claims. His is the third of a trio of essays on validity. Cf. the first article by S. W. Van Heerden, "Validity in Old Testament and Biblical Theology." *OTE* 3.2 (1990): 121–31; and the second by H. L. Bosman, which investigates B. S. Childs' work, "The Validity of Biblical Theology: Historical Description or Hermeneutical 'Childs' Play?" *OTE* 3.2 (1990): 133–46.

All three are valuable in giving attention, though definitely not in a thoroughgoing fashion, to matters of epistemology, the verification principle, and the like.

146 R. B. Robinson. "Narrative Theology and Biblical Theology." Pp. 129–42 in *The Promise and Practice of Biblical Theology* (#50). Narrative theology à la Hans Frei asserts a clarity and self-interpreting quality for Scripture. Robinson traces the significance of narrative theology, described as a restorative movement, for biblical theology.

147 B. C. Ollenburger. "From Timeless Ideas to the Essence of Religion: Method in Old Testament Theology before 1930." *FOTT*, pp. 3–19.
Traces the development of OT theology, starting from the nineteenth century, with emphasis on ideas, philosophy, and reason (L. F. Baumgarten-Crusius, W. M. L. de Wette, G. P. Kaiser, J. K. Vatke). A subsequent period, marked by salvation history (e.g., J. C. K. von Hofmann), was followed by attention to the "essence" of a religion (W. Eichrodt).

148 R. P. Knierim. "The Method of Old Testament Theology." Pp. 71–85 in *The Task of Old Testament Theology* (#57).
The method is essentially one of comparison. Examines unsuitable criteria for such comparison, and then outlines constructive criteria. The essay is one of four lectures on biblical theology presented in Brazil.

149 B. C. Ollenburger. "Old Testament Theology: A Discourse on Method." Pp. 81–103 in *Biblical Theology: Problems and Perspectives* (#58).
Describes Gabler's aims and strategies, which are closely related to his understanding of the function of biblical theology vis-à-vis dogmatic theology. Outlines components of a formal method; interacts with J. J. Collins, P. Trible, and Karl Rahner.

150 R. Schultz. "Integrating Old Testament Theology and Exegesis: Genre and Canonical Issues." Pp. 185–205 in *NIDOTTE*. Vol. 1. (#32).

Stresses that the theology of any passage be consistent with the theology of the book (the formulation of which he elaborates via genre, thematic emphasis, etc.) and the canon.

4.4 History and Faith

The program for a history-oriented biblical theology was enunciated by Gabler. The question was in part how to formulate a theology that would arrive at universals, albeit from the particularities of a specific history. By the middle of the nineteenth century, the Erlangen School, particularly J. C. K. von Hofmann, championed Heilsgeschichte (salvation history). In this view, while the whole of human life (history) is in some sense within God's control, certain events as incursions of God on the human plane are of special importance in God's plan for human redemption. Von Rad (so G. F. Hasel) essentially took salvation history as an organizing principle for his theology.

The Biblical Theology Movement in the mid-twentieth century, as represented by G. E. Wright, placed to the fore events, and history generally in formulating a theology. There are several questions. How does one derive theology from narrative? How are faith and theology related to events? In what way are events revelatory of God?

Among those who have exposited or summarized the issues are Barr (see entries in this section), Reventlow (#102, pp. 59–124), and Hasel (#95, pp. 115–38).

151 F. Baumgärtel. "The Hermeneutical Problem of the Old Testament." Pp. 134–59 in *EOTH* (#43). Original Title: "Das alttestamentliche Geschehen als 'heilsgeschichtliches' Geschehen." Pp. 13–28 in *Geschichte und Altes Testament. Aufsätze von W.F. Albright et al.* Beiträge zur historischen Theologie, 16. Tübingen, 1953.

Holds that neither the "confessed" nor the "critical" history of the OT holds theological relevance since the OT is a "witness out of a non-Christian religion" (p. 135).

152 L. Gilkey. "Cosmology, Ontology, and the Travail of Biblical Language." *JR* 41.3 (1961): 194–205.

With G. E. Wright and B. Anderson in mind, Gilkey critiques the Biblical Theology Movement. Gilkey examines the ambiguities that arise when theological language, both biblical and orthodox (e.g., God acts), is used in the framework of a worldview or cosmology that is modern (where language is not universal but analogous). An important article.

153 J. Barr. "Revelation through History in the Old Testament and in Modern Thought." *Int* 17 (1963): 193–205.
Challenges the "God who Acts" theology, noting that God also speaks.

154 A. J. Ehlen. "Old Testament Theology as Heilsgeschichte." *Concordia Theological Monthly* 35 (1964): 517–44.
This helpful survey begins with the Bible's own understanding of history. Ehlen exposits the view on Heilsgeschichte held by J. C. K. von Hofmann and J. T. Beck, and traces its renascence in the twentieth century, noting practitioners such as G. E. Wright and C. Westermann. Cf. F. Hesse. "Abschied von der Heilsgeschichte." *ThSt* 108. Zürich, 1971.

155 R. Rendtorff. "The Concept of Revelation in Ancient Israel." Translated by David Granskou. Pp. 23–53 in *Revelation as History*. Edited by W. Pannenberg. New York: Macmillan, 1968. British Edition: 1969. Original Title: "Die Offenbarungsvorstellungen im Alten Israel." Pp. 21–41 in *Offenbarung als Geschichte*. Edited by W. Pannenberg. Göttingen: Vandenhoeck und Ruprecht, 1961. Second Edition: 1963.
Thesis: In the OT God reveals himself primarily in history. The debate turns about revelation, word, and event. A summary of the larger debate is found in J. M. Robinson. "Revelation as Word and as History." Pp. 42–62 in *Theology as History: New Frontiers in Theology*. Vol. 3. Edited by J. M. Robinson and J. B. Cobb Jr. New York: Harper & Row, 1967.

156 G. F. Hasel. "The Problem of History in OT Theology." *AUSS* 8 (1970): 23–50.
Investigates von Rad's understanding of history, noting also the views of F. Hesse, F. Baumgärtel, and W. Pannenberg.

157 G. E. Wright. "Historical Knowledge and Revelation." Pp. 279–303 in *Translating and Understanding the Old Testament: Essays in Honor of Herbert G. May*. Edited by H. T. Frank and W. L. Reed. Nashville: Abingdon, 1970.
Shows how Luther and Calvin emphasized revelation that had as its content saving truth. Revelation belongs to the realm

of historical knowledge, which is conveyed by narrative. Wrestles with what is meant by revelation.

158 J. Barr. "Story and History in Biblical Theology." *JR* 56 (1976): 11–17. Reprinted in Barr's *Scope and Authority of the Bible.* Philadelphia: Westminster, 1981, pp. 1–17; British Edition: *Explorations in Theology,* 7. London: SCM, 1980, pp. 1–17.

Examines the meaning and implications of replacing the "historical model" with "story." Cf. his "Historical Reading and the Theological Interpretation of Scripture." Pp. 30–51 in *Explorations,* and esp. "Revelation in History." Pp. 746–49 in *IDBS.*

159 W. Herberg. "Biblical Faith as 'Heilsgeschichte': The Meaning of Redemptive History in Human Existence." Pp. 32–43 in *Faith Enacted as History: Essays in Biblical Theology.* Edited by B. W. Anderson. Philadelphia: Westminster, 1976.

Herberg, a Jew, maintains that the fundamental historical movement within the Bible is that of the story of God's activity to accomplish his saving purpose. The essay might be paired with "Five Meanings of the Word 'Historical'" in the same volume, pp. 132–37.

160 A. H. J. Gunneweg. *Understanding the Old Testament.* The Old Testament Library. Translated by John Bowden. Philadelphia: Westminster/London: SCM, 1978. Original Title: *Vom Verstehen des Alten Testaments. Eine Hermeneutik.* Das Alte Testament Deutsch, Ergänzungsreihe Band, 5. Göttingen: Vandenhoeck und Ruprecht, 1977.

Chapter 3 (pp. 43–95) insists on the gap between history and theology and, though sympathetic to the approach, describes difficulties of past attempts to treat the history of Israel's religion as a theology of the OT. Cf. "The Old Testament as History Book" (chap. 4) with discussions about salvation history, typology, and the two Testaments.

161 J. J. Collins. "The 'Historical' Character of the Old Testament in Recent Biblical Theology." *CBQ* 41 (1979): 185–204.

Reviews the positions on history (and factual accuracy) taken by R. de Vaux, G. E. Wright, and G. von Rad, analyzes the history-like character of OT narratives, and questions the commonplace contrast between Near Eastern myth and OT narrative.

162 W. E. Lemke. "Revelation through History in Recent Theology: A Critical Appraisal." *Int* 36.1 (1982): 34–46.

"The concept of revelation through history is not simply a passing theological fad or aberration, but belongs to the core of biblical religion."

163 J. J. Collins. "Biblical Theology and the History of Israelite Religion." Pp. 16–32 in *Back to the Sources: Biblical and Near Eastern Studies.* Dermot Ryan Festschrift. Edited by K. J. Cathcart and J. F. Healey. Dublin: Glendale, 1989.

Urges a socio-historical approach as distinct from the canonical approach. Uses Daniel to illustrate the importance of the literary and the historical contexts; addresses the problems of pseudepigraphy, the portrayal of God, and the hope for resurrection.

164 R. Gnuse. *Heilsgeschichte as a Model for Biblical Theology: The Debate Concerning the Uniqueness and Significance of Israel's World View.* College Theology Society Studies in Religion, 4. Lanham, Md.: University Press of America, 1989.

Rehearses the views of the advocates of Heilsgeschichte and its critics. Investigates the historiography and basic religious values in the ANE and the Bible. Any reconstruction of a salvation history model must come to grips with ANE material. Each chapter has a pithy conclusion. Amply footnoted. An important contribution.

165 J. Strange. "Heilsgeschichte und Geschichte." *SJOT* 2 (1989): 100–113.

Argues that the traditional concept of salvation history is not viable since to be credible it must be identical with history. In a follow-up article, "Geschichte und Heilsgeschichte: Mehrere Aspekte der biblischen Theologie." *SJOT* 2 (1989): 114–35, N. P. Lemche offers a divergent view and shows, using examples, the problems with Strange's position.

166 U. Mauser. "Historical Criticism: Liberator or Foe of Biblical Theology?" Pp. 99–113 in *The Promise and Practice of Biblical Theology* (#50).

Argues that a biblical theology based on historical events has a chance again, but in ways different than in the Biblical Theology Movement.

167 E. A. Martens. "The Oscillating Fortunes of 'History' within Old Testament Theology." Pp. 313–40 in *Faith, Tradition, and His-*

tory: Old Testament Historiography in Its Near Eastern Context. Edited by A. R. Millard, J. K. Hoffmeier, and D. W. Baker. Winona Lake, Ind.: Eisenbrauns, 1994.

Surveys sixty years of theologizing, noting how dominant or recessive the subject of " history" has been in formulating an OT theology. Identifies three approaches, ranging from close attention to history to history as tangential to theology. Opts for a view similar to Westermann's, where history is the primary but not exclusive datum for theology.

168 L. Perdue. *The Collapse of History: Reconstructing Old Testament Theology.* OBT. Minneapolis: Fortress, 1994.

Traces the shift from the historical model of doing OT theology, beginning with Wright's event-oriented *God Who Acts* (#258) and von Rad's tradition-oriented approach (#268), moving through Gottwald's liberation model, to other models, such as creation/Wisdom model, canon (Childs [#293] and [#303]), metaphor (Sally McFague), and the literary models of story and imagination. Each modality is illustrated using Jeremiah.

169 R. P. Knierim. "Cosmos and History in Israel's Theology." Pp. 171–224 in *The Task of Old Testament Theology* (#57).

An essay indicative of the shift from a preoccupation with history to a focus on world order, creation, and cosmology. Discusses the relationship among election, creation, and history.

4.5 The Place of Wisdom

Especially for a theological approach basing itself on Heilsgeschichte, the incorporation of Wisdom material has represented a challenge. G. E. Wright described Wisdom material in the flow of Old Testament material as a cul-de-sac. Some scholars, such as S. Terrien (#282), have regarded Wisdom as more central. J. Høgenhaven (#106) has proposed that in organizing OT theology, Wisdom materials be given a lead position. Items listed in this category discuss primarily the questions pertaining to Wisdom material in formulating an OT theology. For the theology of the Wisdom corpora, see §7.5.

170 J. F. Priest. "Where Is Wisdom to Be Placed?" *JAAR* 31 (1963): 275–82. Reprinted in *Studies in Ancient Israelite Wisdom*, pp. 281–88. Edited by J. L. Crenshaw. New York: KTAV, 1976.

Argues that there existed a common religious tradition in early Israel from which prophets, priests, and wise men selected specific emphases without necessarily rejecting those emphases chosen by other groups (p. 281).

171　W. Zimmerli. "The Place and Limit of the Wisdom in the Framework of the Old Testament Theology." *SJT* 17 (1964): 146–58. Reprinted in *Studies in Ancient Israelite Religion*, pp. 314–26. Edited by J. L. Crenshaw. New York: KTAV, 1976.
　　　Wisdom "thinks resolutely within the framework of a theology of creation. . . . In the framework of an Old Testament Theology, the sapiential theology of creation will be recalled to the God who joined Himself to His people by His encounter with them in history" (p. 158).

172　J. Harvey. "Wisdom Literature and Biblical Theology. " *BTB* 1 (1971): 308–19.
　　　Reviews H. H. Schmidt's *Wesen und Geschichte der Weisheit: Untersuchung zur altorientalischen und israelitischen Weisheitsliteratur.* BZAW, 101. Berlin, 1966.

173　G. von Rad. *Wisdom in Israel.* Nashville: Abingdon, 1972.
　　　A renowned biblical theologian describes Israel's Wisdom as a form of Yahwism with a trust in the orders and attention to pragmatic instruction.

174　W. C. Kaiser Jr. "Wisdom Theology and the Centre of Old Testament Theology." *EQ* 50 (1978): 132–46.
　　　Argues that the fear of God brings law and Wisdom together; both can be integrated into the unifying OT theme of promise. C. H. H. Scobie describes such a connection as a "slender thread."

175　J. Goldingay. "The 'Salvation History' Perspective and the 'Wisdom' Perspective within the Context of Biblical Theology." *EvQ* 51 (1979): 194–207.
　　　Wisdom is not a subset of salvation but its complement. Wisdom is preoccupied with creation; salvation history, with redemption.

176　S. Terrien. "The Play of Wisdom: Turning Point in Biblical Theology." *HBT* 3 (1981): 125–53.
　　　Takes the view that the theological field of force that accounts for canonical literature is not so much covenant or Deuteronomic theology as it is divine presence. Personified Wisdom,

playful in God's presence, speaks to the tension of Torah and Prophets and is the pivot in the growth of the canon.

177 C. H. H. Scobie. "The Place of Wisdom in Biblical Theology." *BTB* 14 (1984): 43–48.

Reviews the place of Wisdom in several OT theologies. Advocates attention to Wisdom and biblical themes, such as creation and history, theology and ethics, male and female.

178 G. V. Smith. "Is There a Place for Job's Wisdom in Old Testament Theology?" *TrinJ* 13 (1992): 3–20.

Offers reasons why Wisdom has been excluded from some OT theologies, shows how it has been incorporated in others, and, illustrating from Job (and comparing with Proverbs and Ecclesiastes), arrives at a central theme for Wisdom: God rules over Israel, the nations, and nature—a thematic that has a place in OT theology.

179 R. E. Murphy. "Wisdom Literature and Biblical Theology." *BTB* 24 (1994): 4–7.

This article explores the female character of Israelite Wisdom as a balance to the culturally conditioned language of biblical patriarchalism. Also notes topics of theological relevance (e.g., creation theology, moral function).

180 R. E. Clements. "Wisdom and Old Testament Theology." Pp. 269–86 in *Wisdom in Ancient Israel: Essays in Honour of J. A. Emerton.* Edited by J. Day, R. P. Gordon, and H. G. M. Williams. Cambridge: Cambridge University Press, 1995.

Identifies problem aspects of incorporating Wisdom into OT theology. Holds that Wisdom functioned not so much as a body of doctrines, but more as a method of inquiry with a passion for education, and so shaped the literary dimension of Jewish faith as well as how Torah and nurture were understood.

4.6 Center/Unity

In the renaissance of biblical theology following the 1930s, OT theologies, in a concern to demonstrate the essence of Israelite faith, were commonly organized around a center (cf. Eichrodt [#266]; Vriezen). G. von Rad (#268) in identifying the ebb and flow of traditions and the consequent shifting theologies, challenged the possibility of an adequate OT theology structured around a center. The OT, he said, "has not a center *(Mitte)* as is found in the New Testament." The pluralities of theologies, noted others, did not readily accommodate attempts to locate a "center." One must speak, therefore, of a unity forged via interlocking traditions; the language was that of trajectories and boundaries rather than "center." By the end of the twentieth century, a consensus of sorts emerged questioning the viability of a center. Absence of a "center" could, but need not, call into question the matter of unity.

Convenient summaries of the debate are located in Reventlow (#102) and Hasel (#95). See also dictionary articles. Material relevant to the unity of the OT is found also in §5.1.

181 H. H. Rowley. *The Unity of the Bible.* Philadelphia: Westminster/London: Carey Kingsgate, 1953.

Stresses a dynamic unity around expectation and fulfillment; sees unity between law and prophets. Other subjects: cross, Christian sacraments. Cf. his "The Unity of the Old Testament." *BJRL* 29 (1945–46): 326–58.

182 G. Fohrer. "The Centre of a Theology of the OT." *Nederduitse Gereformeerde Teologiese Tydskrif* 7 (1966): 198–206. A German translation, "Der Mittelpunkt einer Theologie des Alten Testaments" appeared in *TZ* 24 (1968): 161–72.

Proposes twin concepts around which the OT could be grouped, namely, "the rule of God and the communion between God and man" (p. 198).

183 F. C. Prussner. "The Covenant of David and the Problem of Unity in OT Theology." Pp. 17–44 in *Transitions in Biblical Scholarship: Essays in Divinity.* Edited by J. C. Rylaarsdam. Chicago: University of Chicago Press, 1968.

Notes how representative scholars (e.g., Eichrodt, Sellin, Vriezen, Jacob) have dealt with the matter of unity. Proposes that the "Covenant with David," which was a new direction in Israel's faith, together with the royal theology it expressed, was the unifying factor in Israel's faith.

184 R. Smend. *Die Mitte des Alten Testaments.* Theologische Studien, 101. Zurich: EVZ-Verlag, 1970. Article by the same title reprinted in *Die Mitte des Alten Testaments: Gesammelte Studien Band I.* Beiträge zur evangelischen Theologie. Vol. 99. München: Chr. Kaiser, 1986, pp. 40–84.

Disagrees with G. von Rad, who did not occupy himself with looking for a center. Reviews earlier proposals (e.g., covenant, monotheism). Revives as center of the OT a formula proposed by J. Wellhausen: "Yahweh the God of Israel, Israel the people of Yahweh." *Israelitisch-jüdische Religion. Die Kultur der Gegenwart* I/41. Leipzig, 1905. Smend's collected essays include "Die Bundesformel," an article first published in 1963.

185 F. C. Fensham, "The Covenant as Giving Expression to the Relationship between Old and New Testament." *TynBul* 22 (1971): 82–94.

Reviews proposals on how the two Testaments are to be related (e.g., Heilsgeschichte). Suggests on the basis of covenant ritual and covenant terminology that the covenant is a strong link between the Testaments.

186 G. F. Hasel. "The Problem of the Center in the Old Testament Theology Debate." *ZAW* 86 (1974): 65–82.

Reviews the arguments in the debate, examines von Rad's position and subsequent developments. God is the center of the OT, but any single organizing center is likely to be a tour de force.

187 W. C. Kaiser Jr. "The Center of Old Testament Theology: The Promise." *Themelios* 10 (1974): 1–10.

Sees the "key" to the center chiefly in God's tripartite promise to Abraham as given in Genesis 12:1–3.

188 W. Zimmerli. "Zum Problem der 'Mitte' des Alten Testamente." *EvTh* 35 (1975): 97–118.

Seeks to determine what is meant by "center," points to Yahweh as a controlling figure, as illustrated in Wisdom literature but also elsewhere (Exod. 3) and in the prophets.

189 P. D. Hanson. *The Diversity of Scripture: A Theological Interpretation.* OBT. Philadelphia: Fortress, 1982.

Seeks ways of recognizing coherence and unity within diversity by examining twin polarities, such as form/reform (kings and prophets) and vision/pragmatism (apocalyptics and priests).

190 B. Janowski and M. Welder (eds.). *Jahrbuch für Biblische Theologie.* Vol. 1: *Einheit und Vielfelt Biblischer Theologie.* Neukirchen-Vluyn: Neukirchener, 1986.

The first volume of this annual is devoted to the unity/plurality issue. Essays are grouped in three sections: perspectives and problems; interdisciplinary discussion; and a bibliographical section, where a useful bibliography arranged under thirty headings covers the 1982–85 period. P. Stuhlmacher reviews H. Seebass's book, *Der Gott der ganzen Bibel*; H. G. Reventlow reviews M. Oeming's book (#212).

191 W. H. Schmidt. "The Problem of the 'Centre' of the Old Testament in the Perspective of the Relationship between History of Religion and Theology." *OTE* 4 (1986): 44–64. An earlier, shorter version appeared as "Die Frage nach der 'Mitte' des AT im Spannungsfeld der Religionsgeschichte und Theologie." Pp. 55–65 in *Gott loben das ist unser Amt. Festschrift für D. J. Schmidt.* Edited by K. Juergensen et al. Kiel, 1984.

Advocates a religio-historical approach rather than the use of an "underlying fundamental idea" and proposes that the First Commandment speaks both to the peculiarity of the Yahweh faith in relation to neighboring nations and to the unity of the OT.

192 J. Goldingay. *Theological Diversity and the Authority of the Old Testament.* Grand Rapids: Eerdmans, 1987.

Analyzes three approaches to handling theological diversity: (1) different viewpoints are reflecting different contexts, making a synthesis difficult; (2) an evaluative approach tested on Deuteronomy; and (3) a preferred approach, taking seriously the possibility of a center. In the latter a sketch is given around the combined themes of creation and salvation. A very full bibliography makes this a fine book overall. Cf. J. Goldingay, "Diversity and Unity in Old Testament Theology." *VT* 34 (1984): 153–68.

193 J. G. McConville. "Using Scripture for Theology: Unity and Diversity in Old Testament Theology." Pp. 39–57 in *The Challenge of Evangelical Theology: Essays in Approach and Method.* Edited by N. M. de S. Cameron. Edinburgh: Rutherford House Books, 1987. Published as a special study of *Scottish Bulletin of Evangelical Theology* 5 (1987).

Reviews approaches that begin with diversity (e.g., von Rad). Shows the effect of doing exegesis by postulating unity. Notes ingredients for an adequate OT theology: (1) recognition of forward movement; (2) a theological-existential element.

194 W. Dietrich. "Der rote Faden im AT." *EvT* 49 (1989): 232–50. Proposes "righteousness" as both a "center" and a bridge to the NT. Develops H. Seebass's suggestion in "Gerechtigkeit Gottes, Zum Dialog mit Peter Stuhlmacher." Pp. 115–34 in *Jahrbuch für Biblische Theologie* (#37).

195 D. P. Fuller. "The Importance of a Unity of the Bible." Pp. 63–75
in *Studies in Old Testament Theology* (#53).
   "[The] Bible's unity is found in the goal intended by the
sequence and climax of its redemptive events" (p. 65). Cf.
Fuller's book, *The Unity of the Bible: Unfolding God's Plan
for Humanity.* Grand Rapids: Zondervan, 1992.

5

Perspectives on Old Testament Theology

Aside from distinct issues of definition, task, and methodology within the discipline of OT theology, there are related perspectives from which the enterprise can be viewed. The discipline reaches its tentacles into many areas. So, for example, one might ask what consideration should be given to the NT in constructing an OT theology. How do Jewish interests impinge on an OT theology? What contribution can OT theology make to Christian preaching? In this category the entries are definitely more suggestive than exhaustive; besides, the classification boundaries easily blur.

5.1 Biblical Theology: Canon, OT, NT

Since the time of G. L. Bauer in 1796 (#245), biblical theologies have followed the lines of scholarly specialization in either OT or NT. Biblical theologies incorporating the entire Bible are rare and can be counted on two hands, said John Reumann as late as 1991 (#50). Such comprehensive theologies have not been listed separately here, but, since they include the Old Testament, are incorporated in chapter 6.

Entries in this section generally address the desirability or the "problematic" of a panbiblical theology, or suggest how a more comprehensive biblical theology incorporating both Testaments might be forged. Some entries in this classification move beyond the question of the connectedness of the two Testaments to the Christian use of the OT, though that subject is taken up more fully in §5.4.

A detailed bibliographic survey of the relationship between OT and NT, between Israel and the church, is presented in Reventlow (#213). Mention should be made of the annual *Jahrbuch für Biblische Theologie* (#37, cf. #190), which is dedicated to discussions inclusive of both Testaments. An overview on the relationship between the two Testaments is found in Hasel (#95, pp. 172–93). For an earlier discussion, see Harrington (#96, pp. 260–404).

196 E. G. Kraeling. "Toward a Biblical Theology?" Pp. 265–84 in *The Old Testament since the Reformation* (#121).

Reviews the Eissfeld–Eichrodt debate and comments on subsequent OT theologies by E. Sellin, L. Köhler, W. Eichrodt, O. Procksch, G. von Rad, G. E. Wright, F. Baumgärtel, and others.

197 B. W. Anderson (ed.). *The Old Testament and Christian Faith: A Theological Discussion* (#42).

Essays on the significance of the OT for the Christian faith are presented by R. Bultmann, Alan Richardson, J. L. McKenzie, and Emil Brunner. Cf. in the same volume C. Westermann, "The Way of Promise through the Old Testament" and B. W. Anderson, "The New Covenant and the Old."

198 C. Westermann (ed.). *Essays on Old Testament Hermeneutics* (#43).

The essays in this volume by G. von Rad, Zimmerli, Eichrodt, and Bultmann bear on ways to see the relationship between the OT and NT.

199 R. E. Murphy. "The Relationship between the Testaments." *CBQ* 26 (1964): 349–59.

Reviews the debate centered in Bultmann's views, and touches on major positions represented in *EOTH* and *OTCF*; brief considerations on typology, promise, and fulfillment.

200 J. Barr. *Old and New in Interpretation: A Study of the Two Testaments*. London: SCM/New York: Harper & Row, 1966.

The Currie Lectures, given in 1964 at the Austin Presbyterian Theological Seminary, Texas. Gives priority to OT, but moves away from history-centered values in doing theology; treats typology and allegory. The unity of the two Testaments lies in the same God at work in each.

201   A. A. Van Ruler. *The Christian Church and the Old Testament.*
Translated by G. W. Bromiley. Grand Rapids: Eerdmans, 1966,
1971. Translated from a Dutch manuscript by H. Keller into German. Original Title: *Die christliche Kirche und das Alte Testament.* Munich: Kaiser Verlag, 1955.

Notable for the claim that the OT has *theological* priority over
the NT; the view is an alternative to R. Bultmann and
W. Vischer. Israel is more important than the church and the
OT is more important than the NT. Christian preaching must
be about the kingdom of God as well as about Christ. Cf. the
extensive summary (pp. 119–40) in Baker (#204).

202   H. Gese. "Erwägungen zur Einheit der biblischen Theologie."
ZTK 67 (1970): 417–36. Reprinted in his *Vom Sinai zum Zion:
alttestamentliche Beiträge zur biblischen Theologie, Beiträge
zur evangelischen Theologie.* Theologische Abhandlungen, 64.
Munich: Chr. Kaiser Verlag, 1974, pp. 11–30.

Holds that the coherence of a biblical theology, à la von Rad,
lies in the tradition-building process, construed as revelation,
evident in the OT, and continuing and concluding in NT times
with Jesus.

203   H.-J. Kraus. *Die Biblische Theologie: Ihre Geschichte und Prob-
lematik.* Neukirchen-Vluyn: Neukirchener Verlag, 1970.

The history is limited to the continental theologians. Kraus
explores how OT and NT theologies might relate to each other
and to a biblical theology. The final chapters of this 400-page
book address problems and perspectives.

204   D. L. Baker. *Two Testaments, One Bible: A Study of Some Modern Solutions to the Theological Problem of the Relationship
between the Old and New Testaments.* Leicester: InterVarsity,
1976; Downers Grove: InterVarsity, 1977. Second (much revised)
Edition with the subtitle, "A Study of the Theological Relationship between the Old and New Testaments." Downers Grove:
InterVarsity, 1991.

Exceedingly useful as a starting point or summary of the topic.
Reviews proposed solutions: (1) that the OT is the essential
Bible (Van Ruler); (2) that the NT is the essential Bible (Bult-
mann); (3) that OT and NT are equally Christian Scripture
(Vischer); and (4) that OT and NT are one salvation history
(G. von Rad). Lists three themes by which the unity may be
understood: typology, promise and fulfilment, and tension
between continuity and discontinuity. The first edition has

an extensive summary of typology. The second edition, restructured and incisive, features brief summaries of recent theologies, but omits many of the informative footnotes of the first edition.

205 C. Westermann. *Blessing in the Bible and the Life of the Church.* OBT. Translated by Keith Crim. Philadelphia: Fortress, 1978. Original Title: *Der Segen in der Bibel und im Handeln der Kirche.* München: Chr. Kaiser Verlag, 1968.

A renowned OT theologian examines blessing as a divine activity (distinguished from deliverance) in OT and NT.

206 L. Sabourin. *The Bible and Christ: The Unity of the Two Testaments.* New York: Alba House, 1980.

Shows the relevance of covenant and promise to the topic, and elaborates on the prefigurations of Christ in the OT. Extensive bibliography.

207 H. Gese. *Essays on Biblical Theology* (#48).

Several themes, such as death, atonement, and Messiah, are traced from the OT into the NT.

208 B. S. Childs. "Some Reflections on the Search for a Biblical Theology." *HBT* 4.1 (1982): 1–12.

Traces the concern for a biblical theology historically, notes the stimulus for the discipline from the academy and the church, and identifies certain problems for the discipline.

209 G. F. Hasel. "Biblical Theology: Then, Now and Tomorrow." *HBT* 4.1 (1982): 61–93.

Reviews the attempts toward a theology of the total Bible as represented by the traditio-historical method (e.g., H. Gese and Peter Stuhlmacher), the thematic-dialectical approach (e.g., S. Terrien), and especially canonical theology (B. S. Childs).

210 H. Seebass. *Der Gott der ganzen Bibel.* Biblische Theologie zur Orientierung im Glauben. Freiburg/Basel/Wien: Herder Verlag, 1982.

Beginning with the NT assertion that God was in Christ, Seebass moves to the messianic perspectives of the OT, the topics of God's people, God's kingdom, and God as Creator, to come to the crux of his concern: suffering as represented in the Bible and in the Holocaust.

211 W. Zimmerli. "Biblical Theology." *HBT* 4.1 (1982): 95–130.

Stresses that the OT and NT point to one single and distinct
God. Several themes are adduced which, despite transforma-
tions, are manifestations of one common faith.

212 M. Oeming. *Gesamtbiblische Theologien der Gegenwart: Das
Verhältnis von AT und NT in der hermeneutischen Diskussion
seit Gerhard von Rad.* Stuttgart: Kohlhammer, 1985. Second Edition: 1987.
A Bonn dissertation that critiques von Rad on the basis of
H. G. Gadamer's philosophical hermeneutics. A critical review
follows of the works of H. Gese, P. Stuhlmacher, A. H. J. Gunneweg, and B. S. Childs. Notes the tension between a lexical-
historical approach and a theologically evaluative one. The
second edition adds a four-page postscript and some supplementary bibliography. Cf. the six essays grouped under Biblische Theologie in *Altes Testament und christliche Verkündigung.* FS. A. H. J. Gunneweg. Edited by M. Oeming and
A. Graupner. Stuttgart: W. Kohlhammer, 1987.

213 H. G. Reventlow. *Problems of Biblical Theology in the Twentieth Century.* Translated by John Bowden. Philadelphia: Fortress/
London: SCM, 1986. Original Title: *Hauptprobleme der biblischen Theologie im 20 Jahrhundert.* Erträge der Forschung 203.
Darmstadt: Wissenschaftliche Buchgesellschaft, 1983.
A major part (120 pp.) treats the core issue, "The Relationship
of the Old Testament and the New." Dense with bibliographic
references. Cf. #102.

214 C. Westermann. "Zur Frage einer Biblischen Theologie." *JBTh*
1 (1986): 13–30.
This is a lead essay for an issue devoted to "Einheit und Vielfalt
Biblischer Theologie." Discusses the continuities and dis-
continuities between the Testaments. Other essays by H. Seebass, P. Stuhlmacher, and M. Oeming take up God's righteousness, knowledge of God, and unity of Scripture. The
bibliography on biblical theology from 1982 to 1985 consists
primarily of German works.

215 H. Hübner. *Biblische Theologie des Neuen Testaments. Prolegomena,* vol. 1, *Die theologie des Paulus,* vol. 2. Göttingen: Vandenhoeck und Ruprecht, 1990, 1993.
The first of three projected volumes discusses methodological issues, among them an extended section on the relationship of the OT and NT. Radically differentiates the God of the
OT from the God of the NT. In a most nonconventional way

Hübner limits himself to that part of the OT quoted by the NT. Cf. the response by B. S. Childs. "Die Bedeutung der hebräischen Bibel für die biblische Theologie." *TZ* 48 (1992): 382–90.

216 C. H. H. Scobie. "The Challenge of Biblical Theology." *TynBul* 42.1 (1991): 31–61. "The Structure of Biblical Theology." *TynBul* 42.2 (1991): 163–93.

Reviews recent developments (e.g., canonical-biblical theology) as a prelude to his own proposal, one that would be multithematic and dialectic, built around God's order, God's servant, God's people, and God's way. Cf. his "New Directions in Biblical Theology." *Themelios* 17 (1992): 4–8.

217 C. H. H. Scobie. "Three Twentieth Century Biblical Theologians." *HBT* 14 (1992): 51–69.

Burrows (#253), Terrien (#282), and Seebass (#288), each of whom attempted a theology that embraced both Testaments, are assessed vis-à-vis scope, structure, and methodology. The more imaginative aspects of Terrien and Seebass are praised.

218 W. J. Wessels. "Biblical Theology: A Challenge to Biblical Scholars." *Scriptura* 40 (1992): 30–39.

Proposes to move away from the idea of a center for writing OT and NT theology. Instead, in working toward a theology of the whole Bible, suggests concentrating on themes and topics. Matters of canon and the relationship between the two Testaments also come into play.

219 S. Pedersen. *New Directions in Biblical Theology.* Papers of the Aarhus Conference, 16–19 September 1992. Supplements to *Novum Testamentum* 76. Leiden: E. J. Brill, 1994.

While most of the thirteen essays have a NT orientation (e.g., "Biblische Theologie im Römerbrief"), the book, as the Scripture and author indexes suggest, also engages OT theologians.

220 J. H. Charlesworth. "What Has the Old Testament to Do with the New?" Pp. 39–87 in *The Old and New Testaments: Their Relationship and the "Intertestamental" Literature.* Edited by J. H. Charlesworth and W. P. Weaver. Valley Forge, Pa.: Trinity, 1993.

Scans the views of Eichrodt (covenant), von Rad (typology), Childs (canon), Sanders (Torah as canon), and Terrien (presence). Favors the promise–fulfilment paradigm, which might better be labeled promise–expectation; typology remains one of several connectors.

221 R. Rendtorff. "The Importance of the Canon for a Theology of the Old Testament." Pp. 46–56 in *Canon and Theology* (#55).

Discusses the final form of biblical books, the development of the canon in Jewish history, and the relationship between the Jewish and the Christian canon. Cf. G. J. Brooke, "The Qumran Scrolls and Old Testament Theology" (#59).

222 R. P. Knierim. "The Old Testament, the New Testament, and Jesus Christ." Pp. 123–38 in *The Task of Old Testament Theology* (#57).

Notes how the two Testaments are often set against each other. However, a biblical theology must account for God's reign just as much as Christ's reign. Cf. pp. 550–54 in the same volume.

5.2 The Jewish Perspective

Since the Jewish people regard the so-called OT as their Scripture, and since the dialogue between Christians and Jews has increased, the question of how the Jewish interpreters relate to OT theology has recently become more acute.

223 J. Blenkinsopp. "Old Testament Theology and the Jewish–Christian Connection." *JSOT* 8 (1984): 3–15.

Notes the failure of OT theologies to incorporate sapiential material adequately, the Christian–Jewish alienation even if unintended, the limitations of the Heilsgeschichte approach, and suggests a re-visioning of early Christianity within the matrix of Judaism.

224 M. Tsevat. "Theology of the Old Testament—A Jewish View." *HBT* 8.2 (1986): 33–50.

Notes the absence of Jewish attempts at OT theology due to the Jewish practice of reading the OT through the lens of the Talmud. Posits that Paul was one of the first OT theologians. B. W. Anderson responds, pp. 51–59.

225 M. H. Goshen-Gottstein. "Tanakh Theology: The Religion of the Old Testament and the Place of Jewish Biblical Theology." Pp. 617–44 in *Ancient Israelite Religion: Essays in Honor of Frank Moore Cross.* Edited by P. D. Miller, P. D. Hanson, and S. D. McBride. Philadelphia: Fortress, 1987.

By a professor at Hebrew University–Jerusalem, who has for
more than a decade explored the theology of the Law, the
Prophets, and the Writings. Sketches what a Jewish biblical
theology would deal with, and suggests some considerations
for method.

226 J. Levenson. "Why Jews Are Not Interested in Biblical Theology." Pp. 281–307 in *Judaic Perspectives in Ancient Israel.* Edited
by J. Neusner, B. Levine, and E. S. Frerichs. Philadelphia: Fortress,
1987.

Cites anti-Semitism, the Protestant preoccupation with *sola
Scriptura,* and a propensity toward systematic theology as well
as a disregard for context as answers to the question. A revised
version appears in J. D. Levenson, *The Hebrew Bible, the Old
Testament and Historical Criticism: Jews and Christians in
Biblical Studies.* Louisville: Westminster/John Knox, 1993,
pp. 33–61.

227 E. Brocke. "Von den 'Schriften' zum 'Alten Testament'—und
zurück? Jüdische Fragen zur christlicher Suche einer 'Mitte der
Schrift.'" Pp. 581–94 in *Die Hebräische Bibel und ihre
zweifache Nachgeschichte.* Rolf Rendtorff Festschrift. Edited
by E. Blum, C. Macholz, and E. W. Stegemann. Neukirchen-
Vluyn: Neukirchener Verlag, 1990.

Holds that the search for a center is a Christian existentialist
endeavor. This essay is the first of eleven in a section labeled
"Christians and Jews."

228 R. Rendtorff. "Old Testament Theology, Tanakh Theology, or
Biblical Theology? Reflections in an Ecumenical Context." *Bib*
73 (1992): 441–51.

Summarizes why there has not been a Jewish theology; shows
how biblical theology would function vis-à-vis OT theology.
Cf. M. Sweeney, "Tanak versus Old Testament: Concerning
the Foundation for a Jewish Theology of the Bible" #59.

5.3 Sociological Perspectives

An awareness of the importance of sociological considerations per-
meated biblical interpretation in the last decades of the twentieth century. Liberation theology (e.g., J. P. Miranda, *Marx and the Bible: A
Critique of the Philosophy of Oppression* [Maryknoll, N.Y.: Orbis,

1974]) and feminist readings, to name but two, shaped the exegesis of biblical texts. Literature on the importance of such readings and essays on biblical texts illustrative of the newer approaches (including literary approaches) is bountiful. However, the further step of constructing integrated OT theologies from these perspectives has not been taken, though discussions about it are under way (e.g., Trible, [#143]).

229 C. J. Pressler. "Feminism and Biblical Theology: A Creative Clash." *Koinonia: Princeton Theological Seminary Graduate Forum* 1 (1989): 19–21.

Discusses the works of Elizabeth Schüssler Fiorenza, Phyllis Trible, and Rosemary Radford Ruether, each of whom shows some affinity with, but more directly offer challenges to traditional biblical theology as represented by Eichrodt, von Rad, Childs, and Brueggemann.

230 I. G. P. Gous. "Old Testament Theology of Reconstruction: Sociocultural Anthropology, Old Testament Theology and a Changing South Africa." *OTE* 6 (1993): 175–89.

Notes the similarity between OT theology and the South African scene, both of which pose the problem of diversity versus unity. Looks to anthropology for some information about the essence of religion. Offers suggestions for a constructive OT theology pertinent to South Africa.

5.4 Christian Preaching

If an OT theology is not as much a descriptive systematization of historically located beliefs as a synthesis normative for a believing community, as some advocate, then its kerygmatic function is at once apparent. An OT theology is not only an academic exercise; it is an exercise to assist the faith community to be faithful to its canon. As has been said, biblical theology functions as does a public health department in behalf of its community. But beyond a monitoring function, an OT theology calls for proclamation, whether through teaching or preaching.

The entries in this category are chosen sometimes for their bibliography, but most often for their awareness of the importance of the biblical-theological component in preaching the OT. Hence collections of sermons such as H. W. Wolff's *The Old Testament and Christian Preaching* (Philadelphia: Fortress, 1986), have not been included.

231 E. P. Clowney. *Preaching and Biblical Theology.* Grand Rapids: Eerdmans, 1961.

A slender book (123 pp.) containing four lectures. Defines biblical theology, sees it as furnishing the charter for preaching as well as delineating the content: Jesus Christ.

232 J. Bright. *The Authority of the Old Testament.* Nashville: Abingdon, 1967.

Critiques earlier proposals grounding the authority of the OT. "The key to the Bible's authority, then, lies in its theology" (p. 151). Stresses the "structure of theology that undergirds the OT" (e.g., election, covenant, kingship) as an answer to the Christian's use of the OT.

233 K. H. Miskotte. *When the Gods Are Silent.* Translated by J. W. Doberstein; incorporating author's revisions and additions for the German edition. New York: Harper & Row/London: Collins, 1967. Original Title: *Als de Goden Zwijgen.* Amsterdam: Uitgeversmaatschappij, 1956. German Edition: *Wenn die Götter Schweigen.* Revised and augmented by the author. Munich: Chr. Kaiser Verlag, 1963.

Hailed as one of the most theological German works of the decade. Analyzes the post-Christian era. The orientation is Barthian. Holds that the kingdom is God's ultimate purpose; creation is already a part of God's redemptive history; the two Testaments have the same theology; everything, including the NT in its essence, is already in the OT. Important for conversation between Christians and Jews. Part II deals with the meaning of the OT for our time and hence for preaching.

234 N. Lohfink. *The Christian Meaning of the Old Testament.* Translated by R. A. Wilson. Milwaukee: Bruce, 1968. London: Burns & Oates, 1969. Original Title: *Das Siegeslied am Schilfmeer.* Verlag Josef Knecht, 1965.

Six expositions of themes (e.g., law and grace, death) and pericopes (Exod. 15) are presented with both theological sensitivity and pastoral concern.

235 E. Achtemeier. *The Old Testament and the Proclamation of the Gospel.* Philadelphia: Westminster, 1973.

A recognized OT scholar, who is also a noted preacher, offers a "primer" on the theological content of the Bible (pp. 47–126) and sound suggestions on preaching from the OT.

236 W. C. Kaiser Jr. *The Old Testament and Contemporary Preaching.* Grand Rapids: Baker, 1973.
Six lectures in popular style keying off progressive revelation, especially the "promise doctrine." Addresses the preaching of law, history, prophets, and Wisdom.

237 R. Davidson. "The Old Testament—A Question of Theological Relevance." Pp. 28–43 in *Biblical Studies in Honour of William Barclay.* Edited by J. R. McKay and J. F. Miller. London: Collins, 1976.
Expounds primarily on the theological orientation of Genesis (transcendence) vis-à-vis the view of James Barr.

238 J. Goldingay. *Approaches to Old Testament Interpretation: Issues in Contemporary Theology.* Downers Grove: InterVarsity, 1981. Revised Edition: Apollos imprint, 1990.
Opens with aims of an OT theology; shows how the OT has been appropriated as a faith; a way of life; the story of salvation; witness to Christ; and Scripture. The revised edition updates each section with a helpful bibliography. On the authority of the canon, cf. his *Models for Scripture.* Grand Rapids: Eerdmans/Carlisle: Paternoster, 1994.

239 J. Limburg. "Old Testament Theology for Ministry: The Works of Claus Westermann in English Translation." *Word and World* 1 (1981): 169–78.
Notes Westermann's parish experience, summarizes some of his major works, and offers suggestions for pastors using Westermann's insight on God, creation, and blessing.

240 S. M. Mayo. *The Relevance of the Old Testament for the Christian Faith: Biblical Theology and Interpretative Methodology.* Washington, D.C.: University Press of America, 1982.
A typescript book that deals in an elementary manner with methods, giving a cursory review of literal, allegorical, typological, sensus plenior, and modern critical attempts. Proposes a move from exegesis to principles to application.

241 G. L. Klein (ed.). *Reclaiming the Prophetic Mantle: Preaching the Old Testament Faithfully.* Nashville: Broadman, 1993.
Essays on OT genres (Part I) and the relationship between the two Testaments (e.g., church as Israel, typological exegesis, thematic connectors) (Part II), and helps for sermonizing (e.g., focusing on a biblical theology) (Part III). Does not break new ground, but summarizes the current evangelical position.

242 G. T. M. Prinsloo. "Die rol van Ou Testament Teologie in die
prediking." *Skrif en Kerk* 15 (1994): 358–76.

Gives reasons for the neglect of OT theology in preaching:
(1) problems relating to method, task, and scope of OT theology, and (2) the pastor's inadequate historical and literary
skills. Solutions to both are proposed. OT theology should
function as a bridge between a specific text and today's world,
a proposal Prinsloo illustrates from Numbers 19:1–22. Summarized from *OTA* 18.2 (June 1995), #1083.

243 R. J. Allen and J. C. Holbert. *Holy Roots, Holy Branches: Christian Preaching from the Old Testament.* Nashville: Abingdon,
1995.

Sees the OT as offering "paradigms of God's presence and purposes." Chapter 4 traces four themes: creation, ḥesed, the
deliverance of Israel, and justice. A chapter of sample sermons
is included.

6

Old Testament Theologies

Full-scale OT theologies are listed in this section. These are volumes that offer a synthetic view of the OT. Some are more in the nature of a compendium of themes, but for the most part, the works present a synoptic view. Some do so via a center, while others work genetically or longitudinally. Still others are cast in a dialectic mode.

The first distinct OT theology was produced in the late eighteenth century by G. L. Bauer. In the twentieth century, the first wave of OT theologies came with the publication of W. Eichrodt's works in 1933 (#266). A second wave, largely captured in the term "The Biblical Theology Movement," crested in the 1950s. A third wave of publications came between 1975 and 1990. Toward the end of the century, there was increasing interest in presenting a theology of both Testaments, hence a panbiblical theology, the mode in which the discipline began.

Summaries of several of these theologies may be found in Hasel (#95), Smith (#83), and *FOTT* (#54).

244   C. F. von Ammon. *Entwurf einer reinen biblischen Theologie.* 3 vols. Erlangen: Palm, 1792. Second Edition: 1801–2.
      Set within the framework of Semler's and Lessing's ideology and especially Kant's moral philosophy, the book aspires to a more adequate account of the biblical foundations of dogmatic theology. Assesses the OT from the standpoint of the spirit of the NT, which, it is claimed, is not alien to reason and moral truths *(Wahrheiten).*

245   G. L. Bauer. *The Theology of the Old Testament: Or a Biblical Sketch of the Religious Opinions of the Ancient Hebrews from the Earliest Times to the Commencement of the Christian Era.*

London: Charles Fox, 1838. The English translation is an abbreviation of the German: *Theologie des Alten Testaments: oder Abriss der religiösen Begriffe der alten Hebräer von den altesten Zeiten bis auf den Anfang der christliche Epoche: Zum Gebrauch akademischer Vorlesungen.* Leipzig: Weygand, 1796.

The first distinctly OT theology produced; represents a specialization within biblical theology. Focused on religious ideas and concepts. Bauer distinguished between the particular and the universal, the latter found principally in Proverbs and Job.

246   E. W. Hengstenberg. *Christology of the Old Testament and a Commentary on the Predictions of the Messiah by the Prophets.* 3 vols. Translated by R. Keith. Alexandria, D.C.: William M. Morrison, 1836–39. Edinburgh: T. & T. Clark, 1856–58. Reprinted from the British Edition, 1872–78. Translated by T. Meyer and J. Martin. 4 vols. Grand Rapids: Kregel, 1956. Original Title: *Christologie des Alten Testaments und Commentar über die Messianischen Weissagungen* 1828–35. Second Edition: 1854–57.

This oft-reprinted set by a champion of orthodoxy, though not self-consciously an OT theology, explores a single and unifying theme: messianic prophecies in the Pentateuch but primarily in the Prophets, especially Isaiah and Daniel.

247   G. F. Oehler. *Theology of the Old Testament.* 2 vols. Edinburgh: T. & T. Clark, 1874–75. Revised by G. E. Day of the translation in Clark's Foreign Theological Library, with the additions of the Second German Edition, an Introduction and Notes. Reprinted: New York: Funk & Wagnalls, 1883. Reprinted: Minneapolis: Klock & Klock Christian Publishers, 1978. Reprinted: Grand Rapids: Zondervan, n.d. Original Title: *Theologie des Alten Testaments.* 2 vols. Tübingen, 1873–74. Third Edition: Stuttgart, 1891. An abridgment appears in R. F. Weidner, *Biblical Theology of the Old Testament; based on Oehler.* Second Edition: New York: Revell, 1896.

A large-scale treatment by a conservative German Lutheran, who stresses revelation and the kingdom of God (theocratic kingdom) according to Mosaism, Prophetism, and Wisdom. Oehler approved of Heilsgeschichte, but took creation as his starting point. An enduring book from the nineteenth century.

248   H. Schultz. *Old Testament Theology: The Religion of Revelation in Its Pre-Christian Stage of Development.* 2 vols. Translated by J. A. Paterson from the Fourth German Edition. Edinburgh: T. & T. Clark, 1892. Original Title: *Alttestamentliche Theologie: Die Offenbarungsreligion auf ihrer vorchristlichen Entwickelungsstufe dargestellt.* Frankfurt: Heyder & Zimmer, Second Edition: 1878. Fourth Edition: 1889.

The first volume traces the history of Israel's religion from the pre-Mosaic period to the Greek age of the Maccabees; volume 2 treats the subject synthetically, with discussions on salvation (covenant, atonement), God, man, and hope. Generally considered the best of the nineteenth-century theologians.

249 A. B. Davidson. *The Theology of the Old Testament.* Edinburgh: T. & T. Clark/New York: Charles Scribner, 1904. Reprinted: 1976.

A benchmark book by an Englishman who broke with the prevailing history of religion popular in the late nineteenth century. Edited posthumously, the book is organized essentially around the topics of God, man, and salvation.

250 H. W. Robinson. *Religious Ideas of the Old Testament.* Studies in Theology. London: Duckworth, 1913. Second Edition: revised by L. H. Brockington, 1956.

A British scholar, in this often-reprinted work, utilizes a synthetic approach. The leading ideas are religion itself, God, man, the approach of God to man and man to God, problems of sin and suffering, and hope.

251 E. Sellin. *Theologie des Alten Testaments.* Leipzig: A. Deichert, 1933.

Organized in categories familiar from dogmatics: God, man, and salvation, with an emphasis on God's holiness.

252 H. E. Fosdick. *A Guide to Understanding the Bible: The Development of Ideas within the Old and New Testaments.* New York/London: Harper & Brothers, 1938.

A highly popular work by an influential preacher. Based on the results of higher criticism. Discusses the idea of God, man, right and wrong, immortality, and so on. Hailed by M. Burrows as "by all odds the best book we now have" on the theology of the Bible (#253, p. 331).

253 M. Burrows. *An Outline of Biblical Theology.* Philadelphia: Westminster, 1946.

Written for Christian ministers by a Yale professor. Discussions of twenty-six topics (e.g., revelation, God, Christ, sin, eschatology, the Christian life), which span both Testaments. Valuable for its extensive textual references. Cf. #217.

254 G. Vos. *Biblical Theology: Old and New Testaments.* Toronto: Toronto Baptist Seminary, 1947; Grand Rapids: Eerdmans, 1948.

An early evangelical attempt by a Reformed scholar to include both Testaments under the rubric of "revelation" (Mosaic era, Prophetic era, New Testament era). Limited interaction with other scholarship. Vos became a mentor of C. K. Lehman.

255 O. Baab. *The Theology of the Old Testament.* Nashville: Abingdon, 1949.

Baab "attempts to permit the OT to declare its own faith in its own way" (p. 9). Discusses the validity of a biblical theology. Uses a systematic approach: God, man, sin, salvation, kingdom of God, death and hereafter, and the problem of evil.

256 W. Vischer. *The Witness of the Old Testament to Christ.* Vol. 1: *The Pentateuch.* Translated from the Third German Edition, 1936, by A. B. Crabtree. London: Lutterworth, 1949. Original Title: *Das Christuszeugnis des Alten Testaments.* 2 vols. Zurich/Zollikon: Evangelischer Verlag, 1934–42. Seventh Edition: 1946.

Written against the background of the history of religion. Argues that the relationship between the OT and the NT must be theologically conceptualized, namely, its pointing to Christ. Cf. his article "Everywhere the Scripture Is about Christ Alone." Pp. 90–101 in *OTCF* (#42).

257 O. Procksch. *Theologie des Alten Testaments.* Gütersloh: C. Bertelsmann, 1950.

A posthumous work edited by G. von Rad. In Part A, Procksch treats the history of Israel in the perspective of revelation from a viewpoint that is strongly christological. Part B discusses the conceptual world of the OT: (1) God and world, (2) God and people, and (3) God and man. Eichrodt, his student, acknowledged his debt to Procksch's threefold scheme. Cf. pp. 91–120 in Laurin (#44).

258 G. E. Wright. *God Who Acts: Biblical Theology as Recital.* SBT, 8. Naperville, Ill.: Allenson/London: SCM, 1952. Excerpt in *FOTT,* pp. 100–119.

An influential book in post–World War II North America by Harvard's archaeologist-theologian. Proceeds methodologically via "recital." Highlights the category of history (e.g., exodus) more than doctrinal ideas. While here close to G. von Rad, Wright later aligned himself more nearly with W. Eichrodt (cf. G. E. Wright, *The Old Testament and Theology* [New York:

Harper & Row, 1969], p. 62). His book, *The Old Testament Against Its Environment* (London: SCM, 1950), serves well as an introduction to his theology.

259 J. Bright. *The Kingdom of God: The Biblical Concept and Its Meaning for the Church.* Nashville: Abingdon, 1953.

The noted author of *A History of Israel* traces the unfolding of the concept of the kingdom of God, which "involves in a real sense, the total message of the Bible." Gives primary attention to the OT.

260 P. Heinisch. *Theology of the Old Testament.* Translated by W. G. Heidt. Collegeville, Minn.: Liturgical, 1955. Original Title: *Theologie des Alten Testamentes,* 1940.

Adopts a method comparable to Eichrodt's, looking for the essence of Israel's faith. Organized in five parts: God, creation, human acts, life after death, and redemption. An appendix includes three papal encyclicals on the study of Scripture.

261 L. Köhler. *Old Testament Theology.* Translated by A. S. Todd. Philadelphia: Westminster, 1957. Original title: *Theologie des Alten Testaments.* Tübingen: Verlag von J. C. B. Mohr (Paul Siebeck), 1936.

Organized according to the dogmatic scheme of God, man, and salvation. Numerous word studies.

262 E. Jacob. *Theology of the Old Testament.* Translated by Arthur W. Heathcote and Philip J. Allcock. New York: Harper/London: Hodder & Stoughton, 1958. Original Title: *Théologie de l'Ancien Testament: Revue et augmentée.* Paris/Neuchâtel: Delachaux & Niestlé, 1955. Excerpt in *FOTT,* pp. 148–52.

A French theologian depicts the characteristic aspects of God (names, attributes), often with the use of extensive word studies (e.g., Spirit, righteousness, heart). Highlights especially God's sovereignty as Creator and Lord of history as the unifying theme. Cf. pp. 141–69 in Laurin (#44).

263 T. C. Vriezen. *An Outline of Old Testament Theology.* Translated by S. Neuijen. Boston: Branford/Oxford: Blackwell, 1958. Second Edition: Newton, Mass./Oxford: Blackwell, 1970. Original Title: *Hoofdlijnen der Theologie van het Oude Testament.* Wageningen: Veenman & Zonen, 1949. Second Edition: 1954; Third Edition: 1966. Excerpt in *FOTT,* pp. 82–99.

Argues that communion or "intercourse" between God and humankind constitutes the unifying theme of the OT. Also treats man to man, and God, man, and nature. Opens with a 150-page discussion on the authority of the OT and its appropriation by Christians. Translated into German, Spanish, and Japanese. Cf. pp. 121–40 in Laurin (#44).

264 G. A. F. Knight. *A Christian Theology of the Old Testament.* Richmond: John Knox/London: SCM, 1959. Second Edition: 1964.
Organized in four parts: God; God and creation; God and Israel; the zeal of the Lord. Stresses the importance of purpose in creation and history. Nontechnical but substantive. An appendix discusses "Israel and the Church." Cf. pp. 171–90 in Laurin (#44).

265 R. C. Dentan. *The Design of the Scriptures: A First Reader in Biblical Theology.* New York: Seabury, 1961.
For lay readers. Provides simple commentary on selected passages for thirty-six themes organized broadly under history, doctrine, and life.

266 W. Eichrodt. *Theology of the Old Testament.* 2 vols. Translated by John A. Baker. Philadelphia: Westminster/London: SCM, 1961, 1967. Original Titles: *Theologie des Alten Testaments.* Vol. 1: *Gott und Volk,* 1933; Vol. 2: *Gott und Welt,* 1935; Vol. 3: *Gott und Mensch.* Leipzig: Hinrichs, 1939. Sixth German Edition: Göttingen: Vandenhoeck und Ruprecht, 1959. Excerpt in *FOTT,* pp. 61–78.
A classic, highly influential synthesis of "the essence of Israel's religion" understood as covenant, which "enshrines Israel's most fundamental conviction, namely, its sense of a unique relationship with God." Three parts: God and people; God and world; and God and man. Sensitive to ANE dimensions (though his work was prior to proposals about links between covenant and political treaties) and to connections with the NT. An "Excursus" (1:512–20) interacts with G. von Rad. For summaries and discussion cf. pp. 23–62 in Laurin (#44); Spriggs (#133); Clements (#69); and *TRZ* 9:371–73.

267 P. and E. Achtemeier. *The Old Testament Roots of Our Faith.* Nashville: Abingdon, 1962. Revised Edition: Peabody, Mass.: Hendrickson, 1994.
Rehearses the OT synoptically largely under the theme of promise by noting the successive stages (e.g., narratives in the Pentateuch, covenant, kingship, prophetic understanding).

268 G. von Rad. *Old Testament Theology.* Vol. 1: *The Theology of Israel's Historical Traditions.* Vol. 2: *The Theology of Israel's Prophetic Traditions.* Translated by David M. G. Stalker. New York: Harper & Row/Edinburgh: Oliver & Boyd, 1962, 1965. Original Title: *Theologie des Alten Testaments.* Vol. 1: *Die Theologie der geschichtlichen Überlieferungen Israels.* Vol. 2: *Die Theologie der prophetischen Überlieferungen Israels.* Munich: Kaiser, 1957, 1960. Excerpt in *FOTT,* pp. 123–44.

A stimulating, classic, and highly influential work by a pioneer of form-critical and traditio-historical methodologies in the school of A. Alt. Eschews search for a thematic unity; depicts the surfacing through time of various traditions (e.g., exodus, conquest). Sets forth the kerygma of different OT books or group of books. A "Postscript" comments on method (2:410–29). For summaries and discussion, see Laurin (#44); Spriggs (#133); Clements (#69).

269 J. B. Payne. *The Theology of the Older Testament.* Grand Rapids: Zondervan, 1962.

Uses "testament" as the organizing principle (e.g., the testator: God; the heir: man, etc.). Intriguing charts. This synthesis by a conservative scholar is in many ways influenced by systematic theology. An annotated bibliography.

270 R. Davidson. *The Old Testament. Knowing Christianity.* Philadelphia: Lippincott, 1964.

A nontechnical work whose interest is "that deep unity of thought concerning God and man which is to be found in the diversity of the book of the Old Testament." Employs a topical approach (e.g., God and history, God and worship, God and wisdom, and God and the future).

271 J. N. Schofield. *Introducing Old Testament Theology.* Philadelphia: Westminster, 1964.

A slender volume with brief discussions on the God who acts, the God who speaks, God's kinship with man, and the glory of God.

272 P. Van Imschoot. *Theology of the Old Testament: I. God.* Translated from the French. New York: Desclée, 1965. Original Title: *Théologie de l'Ancien Testament.* 2 vols. Tournai: Desclée, 1954, 1956.

Three volumes were projected around a dogmatic scheme: God, man, and salvation. Two volumes appeared, the first of which was translated into English. A lengthy section on revelation. An important contribution by a Roman Catholic. Cf. pp. 191–215 in Laurin (#44).

273 C. K. Lehman. *Biblical Theology*. Vol. 1: *Old Testament*. Scottdale, Pa., 1971.

Leans heavily on G. Vos. Presents the "unfolding of God's revelation" with close attention to the Mosaic period (includes subjects such as worship and law) and the Prophets (e.g., messianic kingdom, life of the people of God, specific theologies of Isaiah). Concludes with the Hagiographa (Writings).

274 R. Youngblood. *The Heart of the Old Testament*. Grand Rapids: Baker, 1971.

A slender, popularly written book that traces nine key ideas throughout the OT to demonstrate its unity: monotheism, sovereignty, election, covenant, theocracy, law, sacrifice, faith, and redemption. No footnotes or indexes.

275 A. Deissler. *Die Grundbotschaft des Alten Testaments: Ein theologischer Durchblick*. Freiburg: Herder, 1972.

Intended as a student's introductory handbook. Organized around the topic of a solicitous deity, Yahweh (transcendent, personal), a God who involves himself positively with the world and with humankind.

276 G. Fohrer. *Theologische Grundstrukturen des Alten Testaments*. Theologische Bibliothek Töpelmann 24. Berlin/New York: Walter de Gruyter, 1972.

A compact work. Proposed a dual concept for organizing OT theology: the rule of God *(Gottesherrschaft)* and the divine–human communion *(Gottesgemeinschaft)*. The final chapter (pp. 185–273) indicates life applications.

277 F. F. Bruce. *New Testament Development of Old Testament Themes*. Grand Rapids: Eerdmans, 1973. British Edition: *This Is That: The New Testament Development of Some Old Testament Themes*. Exeter: Paternoster, 1968.

Seven essays (ten to twelve pages each) on the rule of God, the salvation of God, the victory of God, the people of God, the Son of God, the Servant Messiah, and the Shepherd King. Popular in tone, but scholarly and informed. Shortchanges the OT.

278 J. L. McKenzie. *A Theology of the Old Testament.* Garden City, N.Y.: Doubleday, 1974. Excerpt in *FOTT*, pp. 170–87.

Treats a variety of themes (e.g., cult, revelation, history, nature, wisdom) without seeking a center and without relating the OT to the NT. The subject of the OT is not a system but a reality—Yahweh. A stimulating work by a prolific Catholic scholar.

279 S. G. De Graaf. *Promise and Deliverance.* 4 vols. Translated by H. Evan Runner and Elisabeth Wickers Runner. St. Catharines, Ont.: Paideia, 1977–81. Original Title: *Verbondsgeschiedenis.* Kampen: J. H. Kok, n.d.

The first two volumes treat the OT. This work offers orientation to teachers of older children in telling Bible stories: God's revelation with themes of covenant and kingdom are to be the frame, rather than human biography. Each chapter has a perspective for the teacher and a retelling of the story.

280 R. E. Clements. *Old Testament Theology: A Fresh Approach.* New Foundations Theological Library. Atlanta: John Knox/London: Marshall, Morgan & Scott, 1978. Excerpt in *FOTT*, pp. 213–32.

With an eye to how Jews and Christians have used the OT (a fresh approach) and sensitivity to the canon (Law and Prophets, also part of the fresh approach), Clements summarizes the OT around the two pervasive themes of Law (Torah) and promise. Good chapters on God and Israel, and the people of God. No discussion of Wisdom.

281 W. C. Kaiser Jr. *Toward an Old Testament Theology.* Grand Rapids: Zondervan, 1978. Excerpt in *FOTT*, pp. 235–53.

Organized around "promise" expounded with its "constellation of terms" (blessing, covenant) through the Bible chronologically. Kaiser leans heavily on Heilsgeschichte. Brief discussion of method. Intended for theologians, pastors, and seminarians. Cf. his own extended summary in "Biblical Theology of the Old Testament." Pp. 328–52 in *Foundations for Biblical Interpretation.* Edited by D. S. Dockery, K. A. Mathews, and R. B. Sloan. Nashville: Broadman & Holman, 1994.

282 S. L. Terrien. *The Elusive Presence: Toward a New Biblical Theology.* Religious Perspectives, 26. San Francisco: Harper & Row, 1978. Excerpt in *FOTT*, pp. 257–75.

Proceeds dialectically: aesthetics/ethics, presence/ absence. Draws on tradition-history, myth and ritual (Scandinavian scholars), and form analysis (German scholars). His discussion encompasses both Testaments (seven chaps. on OT; two on NT), producing a "Hebraic theology of presence" culminating in Jesus (p. 411). The chapter on Wisdom is especially noteworthy.

283   W. Zimmerli. *Old Testament Theology in Outline.* Translated by D. E. Green. Atlanta: John Knox/Edinburgh: T. & T. Clark, 1978. Original Title: *Grundriss der Alttestamentlichen Theologie.* Theologische Wissenschaft, 3. Stuttgart: Kohlhammer, 1972. Second Edition: 1975. Fourth Edition: 1982. Fifth Edition: 1985. Excerpt in *FOTT,* pp. 191–209.

An exegete who majored in source, form, and tradition criticism proposes that the "focal point" of the OT is Yahweh, placing an emphasis on his name and gifts (e.g., land, presence, instruction), but also on the human response. Supplementary essays are collected in *Studien zur alttestamentlichen Theologie und Prophetie.* 2 vols. Theologische Bücherei. Munich: Kaiser, 1963, 1974.

284   W. A. Dyrness. *Themes in Old Testament Theology.* Downers Grove: InterVarsity, 1979.

A standard set of themes, including God, creation, covenant, sin, law, worship, piety, and ethics, are surveyed without an attempt at integration of the themes. Popular in orientation. No footnotes, but has a Scripture index.

285   G. Goldsworthy. *Gospel and Kingdom: A Christian Interpretation of the Old Testament.* Exeter: Paternoster, 1981.

Argues for coherence in biblical revelation via the reality of God's kingdom. A book primarily for pastors and preachers.

286   E. A. Martens. *God's Design: A Focus on Old Testament Theology.* Grand Rapids: Baker, 1981. Second Edition: 1994. British Edition: *Plot and Purpose in the Old Testament.* Leicester: InterVarsity, 1981. Excerpt in *FOTT,* pp. 300–320.

Adopts an exegetical method with Exodus 5:22–6:8 as a pivotal text about God's design, which, in its fourfold components (deliverance, covenant community, knowledge of God, and land/blessing) is unfolded diachronically (pre-monarchy, monarchy, and post-monarchy).

287   N. Lohfink. *Great Themes from the Old Testament.* Translated by R. Walls. Edinburgh: T. & T. Clark, 1982. Original Title:

Unsere grossen Wörter. Das Alte Testament zu Themen dieser Jahre. Freiburg: Herder, 1977.

By means of such themes as pluralism, power, salvation history, liberation, God, leisure, and love, Lohfink desires to "speak of the concern that is common to the Old Testament and to our own times."

288 H. Seebass. *Der Gott der Ganzen Bibel. Biblische Theologie zur Orientierung im Glauben.* Freiburg: Herder, 1982.

Sketches difficulties in doing a biblical theology. Paul's theology is a kind of biblical theology. Discusses motifs of God's creation and God's noninterference. An unconventional approach.

289 C. Westermann. *Elements of Old Testament Theology.* Translated by D. W. Scott. Atlanta: John Knox, 1982. Original Title: *Theologie des Alten Testaments in Grundzügen.* Göttingen: Vandenhoeck und Ruprecht, 1978. Excerpt in *FOTT,* pp. 279–97.

Basing his approach on discussion of events (the coming of the Word of God) rather than concepts (election, covenant), Westermann asks and answers the question, "What does the OT say about God?" He proposes an answer that is verb-dominated (e.g., blessing and saving), but also stresses human response. Elaborates on Wisdom; makes a link with the NT.

290 S. J. De Vries. *The Achievements of Biblical Religion: A Prolegomenon to Old Testament Theology.* Lanham, N.Y.: University Press of America, 1983.

Identifies elements shared by other religions (e.g., awareness of the Holy, a sin-guilt-punishment mechanism) and those that are distinctive (e.g., divine transcendence and immanence; a view of human partnership with God in shaping history; and a monotheistic personalism).

291 W. H. Schmidt. *The Faith of the Old Testament: A History.* Translated by John Sturdy. Philadelphia: Westminster/ Oxford: Basil Blackwood, 1983. Original Title: *Alttestamentlicher Glaube in seiner Geschichte.* Neukirchener Studienbücher Band, 6. Neukirchener Verlag des Erziehungsvereins GmbH, Neukirchen-Vluyn, 1968. Fourth Edition: 1982.

A book "midway between a 'history of Israelite religion' and a 'theology of the Old Testament'" (p. ix). Notes four epochs. Sees the first two commandments as distinctive of Israelite religion.

292 J. Levenson. *Sinai and Zion: An Entry into the Jewish Bible.* Minneapolis: Winston, 1985.

Presents the two foci, Torah and temple, both mountain traditions, from a perspective different than that of the scholarly consensus. Shows openness to rabbinic traditions, as well as to Near Eastern research in elucidating texts. Has been described as "the first Jewish theology of the Hebrew Bible" (J. Goldingay).

293 B. S. Childs. *Old Testament Theology in a Canonical Context.* Philadelphia: Fortress, 1986. Excerpt in *FOTT*, pp. 324–31.

Holds that the object of theological reflection is the canonical writing of the OT (p. 6). Defines and illustrates the canonical approach with certain themes (e.g., law, rituals, functionaries such as prophets and priests). Prominence is given to revelation, especially the law, and human response. Hailed as a "rich and wide-ranging contribution" (Clements).

294 J. Drane. *Old Testament Faith: An Illustrated Documentary.* San Francisco: Harper & Row, 1986.

Definitely an entry-level (high school) work for the nonspecialist by a populizer of the Christian religion. Sample topics: "the living God," "God and the world," "worshipping God."

295 P. D. Hanson. *The People Called: The Growth of the Community in the Bible.* San Francisco: Harper & Row, 1986. Excerpt in *FOTT*, pp. 349–70.

Regards the community nexus for the process of theologizing (understanding of God; community identity) more strategic than the content of faith. Notes the diverse theologies within the OT that give witness to the dynamic activity of God. Follows through into the NT.

296 F. R. McCurley and J. Reumann. *Witness of the Word: A Biblical Theology of the Gospel.* Philadelphia: Fortress, 1986.

Two Lutheran professors address the interplay between the two Testaments. They take as an orientation point Jesus' message of the "gospel of God" and the "kingdom of God," from which perspective they examine the OT in sixteen chapters (170 pages, or one-third of the book).

297 C. Schedl. *Zur Theologie des Alten Testaments. Der Göttliche Sprachvorgang.* Vienna: Herder, 1986.

Delineates OT theology in two parts, around Word and Covenant, as two divine expressions in cosmos and history.

Proceeds methodologically along the lines of a complicated
(and questionable) numerological system described as
"logotechnic."

298 W. A. Van Gemeren. *The Progress of Redemption: The Story of
Salvation from Creation to the New Jerusalem.* Grand Rapids:
Zondervan, 1988.
Each of twelve epochs from creation to the New Jerusalem is
treated synthetically (e.g., literary forms, canonical function)
and related to Jesus and the Scriptures. Written from an evangelical, Reformed perspective.

299 G. Kittel. *Der Name über alle Namen. Biblische Theologie/AT.*
Göttingen: Vandenhoeck und Ruprecht, 1989.
The first of two volumes on biblical theology stressing the
unity of the Bible through the unfolding of certain themes,
predominantly that of God's revelation through his name
(Exod. 3). Four themes follow: freedom, God's uniqueness, a
summons to God's people, and a new future that will embrace
all peoples. Ample documentation; readable.

300 H.-R. Weber. *Power: Focus for a Biblical Theology.* Geneva: World
Council of Churches, 1989.
Traces six biblical trajectories of faith: God's liberating acts,
royal rule, empowering wisdom, holy presence, vindication
of the poor, and renewing judgment. In each chapter the tradition is rehearsed, affirmations of power are both identified
and assessed in the light of Jesus. Subject and Scripture
indexes.

301 M. Strom. *The Symphony of Scripture: Making Sense of the
Bible's Many Themes.* Downers Grove: InterVarsity, 1990.
A walk-through of the OT (twelve chapters) and the NT (nine
chapters) according to periods (e.g., conquest) and genre (e.g.,
Psalms), identifying for each a theme (e.g., holy war, Zion).
Entry-level. Charts. Helps for further studies.

302 C. Barth. *God with Us: A Theological Introduction to the Old
Testament.* Edited by G. W. Bromiley. Grand Rapids: Eerdmans,
1991.
Expounds the main themes of Israel's faith on the grid of God's
mighty acts in word and deed to bring in his kingdom. Nine
such cluster acts are identified. Originally designed for Indone-

sian Christians. Valuable for collation of material (e.g., creation, monarchy), but hardly outstanding.

303 B. S. Childs. *Biblical Theology of the Old and New Testaments: Theological Reflection on the Christian Bible.* Minneapolis: Fortress, 1993. Copyright, 1992.

The leading American biblical theologian's magnum opus. The major section (350 pages) revolves around theological reflection on the Christian Bible. Themes such as God the Creator, Law and gospel, God's kingdom and rule, and the shape of the obedient life: ethics. Not a systematic account of the Bible's teaching. A work of major importance. For an assessment see M. G. Brett. *Biblical Criticism in Crisis: The Impact of the Canonical Approach on Old Testament Studies.* Cambridge: Cambridge University Press, 1991.

304 A. H. J. Gunneweg. *Biblische Theologie des Alten Testaments. Einer Religionsgeschichte Israels in biblischtheologischer Sicht.* Stuttgart: Kohlhammer, 1993.

The approach is historical; devotes separate chapters to different historical periods. Adopts historical critical assumptions. Explores the interrelation between theology and the history of Israel's religion.

305 O. Kaiser. *Der Gott des Alten Testaments. Theologie des Alten Testaments.* Teil 1: Grundlegung. Uni-Taschenbücher für Wissenschaft 1747. Göttingen: Vandenhoeck und Ruprecht, 1993.

A discussion of the task of OT theology is followed by a religio-historical survey. Subjects of God, king, people, and land are examined via the late priestly history, the Deuteronomistic and the Chronistic histories. After a treatment of prophetic and Wisdom material, the conclusion is reached that Torah is the center of the OT. Volume 2 is to follow.

306 R. L. Smith. *Old Testament Theology.* See annotation at #83.

307 J. J. Niehaus. *God at Sinai: Covenant and Theophany.* SOTBT. Grand Rapids: Zondervan, 1995.

Theophanies as the grand organizing theme of the OT are to be understood within a matrix of a hierarchical set of themes: God as King, God's kingdom, God's covenant(s), and God's covenant administered. OT material, including Psalms and Prophets, is treated around the defining Sinai theophany. Considerable attention is given to the ANE; one chapter is devoted to the NT.

308 H. D. Preuss. *Old Testament Theology.* 2 vols. Translated by L. G. Perdue. Louisville: Westminster/John Knox, 1995. Original Title: *Theologie des Alten Testaments.* Vol. 1: *JHWHs erwälendes und verpflichtendes Handeln;* Vol. 2: *Israels Weg mit JHWH.* Stuttgart: W. Kohlhammer, 1991, 1992.

The center *(Mitte)* of the OT lies in the confluence of God's election, thereby obligating Israel. Organized around election, covenant, law, land, and so on. Volume 2 deals with consequences and development of Israel's understanding of divine election, for example, kingship, messianic hope, temple, and prophets. In the second half, the transnational matters of worship and ethics are noted. His work, more descriptive than evaluative and akin to a handbook, has, for its comprehensiveness, been compared to that of Eichrodt and von Rad. Extensive Hebrew vocabulary, subject, and Scripture indexes.

309 J. Schreiner. *Theologie des Alten Testaments.* Die Neue Echter Bibel. Ergänzungsband I. Würzburg: Echter, 1995.

A German Catholic presents ten chapters, the title of each of which contains the word "Yahweh" (e.g., Yahweh, the God of Israel; Yahweh, the saving God; and Yahweh and the future).

7

Theologies of Corpora

In addition to formulating full-scale theologies, scholars in more recent times have summarized major constitutive blocks of the OT theologically. In this section are entries, often essays, which deal with units larger than single biblical books.

7.1 Pentateuch and Pentateuchal Sources

310 H. W. Wolff. "The Kerygma of the Yahwist." *Int* 20 (1966): 131–58. Reprinted in *The Vitality of Old Testament Traditions* (#46), pp. 41–66. German original in *EvTh* 24 (1964): 73–97. Reprinted in Wolff's *Gesammelte Studien zum Alten Testament*. Munich: Chr. Kaiser, 1964, pp. 345–73.

 The kerygma is captured in the word "blessing," understood as an annulment of guilt and constitutive of community life without strife.

311 W. Brueggemann. "The Kerygma of the Priestly Writers." Pp. 109–14 in *The Vitality of Old Testament Traditions* (#46). Reprinted from *ZAW* 84 (1972): 397–413.

 "The kerygmatic key to priestly theology is that the promise of the land of blessing still endures and will be realized soon."

312 T. E. Fretheim. "The Theology of the Major Traditions in Genesis–Numbers." *RevExp* 74.3 (1977): 301–20.

Offers a focus on the theological perspectives of the Yahwistic, Elohistic, and Priestly traditions that were shaped, respectively, in the face of secularization, idolatry, and despair.

313   J. D. W. Watts. "The Deuteronomic Theology." *RevExp* 74.3 (1977): 321–36.
Both Deuteronomy and the Deuteronomistic history were intended to address culture shock—the one of entry into the land, the other of exile.

314   D. J. A. Clines. *The Theme of the Pentateuch.* JSOTSup 10. Sheffield: JSOT, 1978. Reprinted: 1982, 1984, 1986.
Argues for unity from the final form around the theme of "partial fulfilment—which implies also the partial nonfulfilment—of the promise to or blessing (descendants, relationship, land) of the patriarchs" (p. 29). Assesses other "theme" proposals. A slender volume, but amply footnoted.

315   F. H. Gorman Jr. *The Ideology of Ritual Space, Time and Status in the Priestly Theology.* JSOTSup 91. Sheffield: JSOT, 1990.
Specific texts (Exod. 34:29–35; Lev. 14:1–20; 16:8; Num. 19:28–29) are examined in the context of priestly creation theology and a worldview where categories of purity, life/death, the status of the holy, and order/chaos are important.

316   E. H. Merrill. "A Theology of the Pentateuch." Pp. 7–87 in *A Biblical Theology of the Old Testament* (#51).
Genesis 1:16–28 is regarded as foundational: humankind is to rule over the creation. Israel as a priestly nation of covenant functions as a means of regaining the lost privilege of dominion—a perspective from which the theology of each of the five books is outlined.

317   J. H. Sailhamer. "The Mosaic Law and the Theology of the Pentateuch." *WTJ* 53 (1991): 241–61.
Argues that the issue of "faith versus works of the law" was central to the theological purpose of the Pentateuch. Abraham, man of faith, is contrasted (somewhat oddly) with Moses.

318   R. W. L. Moberly. *The Old Testament of the Old Testament: Patriarchal Narratives and Mosaic Yahwism.* OBT. Minneapolis: Fortress, 1992.
A "theological-critical" approach, which examines God's self-disclosure to Moses as Yahweh and differentiates that understanding from patriarchal religion. An exposition that challenges the source-critical position on Pentateuchal composition.

319 N. Lohfink. *Theology of the Pentateuch: Themes of the Priestly Narrative and Deuteronomy.* Translated by L. M. Maloney. Minneapolis: Fortress, 1994. Selection from original titles: *Studien zum Pentateuch* and *Studien zum Deuteronomium und zur deuteronomistischen Literatur.* Stuttgart: Verlag Katholisches Bibelwerk, 1988, 1990.

Not a full-orbed theology but a collection of essays around themes (e.g., connection of creation and salvation) and texts (e.g., Gen. 1:28; Exod. 15:22–27; Deut. 1:6–3:29).

7.2 Former Prophets/Deuteronomic History

320 P. D. Miller. "The Gift of God: The Deuteronomic Theology of the Land." *Int* 23 (1969): 451–65.

"[T]he central theological affirmation about the land is that it is the gift of God to Israel" (p. 453). Basic research is limited to Deuteronomy, but the concept is set in the context of the larger OT and some current agenda.

321 H. W. Wolff. "The Kerygma of the Deuteronomic Historical Work." Pp. 83–100 in *The Vitality of Old Testament Traditions* (#46). German original in *ZAW* 73 (1961): 171–86. Reprinted in H. W. Wolff. *Gesammelte Studien zum Alten Testament.* Munich: Chr. Kaiser Verlag, 1964.

The theme of "return" appears at important high points in the Deuteronomic presentation of history.

322 J. G. McConville. *Grace in the End: A Study in Deuteronomic Theology.* SOTBT. Grand Rapids: Zondervan, 1993.

Builds toward a statement on Deuteronomic theology (chap. 5) by sorting out the views of a range of scholars on the dating and development of the book. The revelation of God in history, election and covenant, and sin and grace are key elements of the theology. A theology of retribution is an inadequate summary.

7.3 Latter Prophets

For the theology of the prophets according to eras (Assyrian period, Babylonian period, Persian period), see von Rad, "Classical Prophecy"

(Part 2). Pp. 129–315 in *Old Testament Theology*, vol. 2 (#268); cf. pp. 238–408 in Lehman (#273).

323 R. E. Clements. *Prophecy and Covenant.* SBT, 43. London: SCM, 1965.
Sees the distinction of the canonical prophets, as contrasted with the nonwriting prophets, to be a preoccupation with the covenant, its demands and promises.

324 E. C. Rust. "The Theology of the Prophets." *RevExp* 74.3 (1977): 337–52.
An unfootnoted article stressing the prophetic consciousness (authority), God (revealed as righteous, sovereign), people of God (sin and judgment), and redemption (remnant, Messiah).

325 R. B. Chisholm Jr. "A Theology of the Minor Prophets." Pp. 397–433 in *A Biblical Theology of the Old Testament* (#51).
The prophetic books are grouped according to centuries—eighth, seventh, sixth/fifth—and their theology is articulated.

326 R. Rendtorff. "The Place of Prophecy in a Theology of the Old Testament." Pp. 57–65 in *Canon and Theology* (#55).
Reviews how G. von Rad and J. Blenkinsopp treat prophets as responding to tradition or as related to the Torah.

7.4 Poetry

327 P. D. Miller. "The Theological Significance of Biblical Poetry." Pp. 211–30 in *Language, Theology, and the Bible* (#56).
After distinguishing between poetry and prose, Miller elaborates on the thesis that "the speaking of God (to, from, and about God) in the Bible is *figural* and *nonliteral;* it is *indirect* and *open*" (p. 225).

7.5 Wisdom

328 G. von Rad. *Wisdom in Israel.* Nashville: Abingdon, 1972. Original Title: *Weisheit in Israel.* Neukirchen-Vluyn: Neukirchener, 1970.
Attempts to "work out some of the specific trends of thought and theological context in which this Israelite wisdom func-

tioned." The book can be read as a supplement to his *Old Testament Theology*, which focused on Heilsgeschichte. Treats several "individual subjects of instruction" (e.g., doctrine of the proper time, the self-revelation of creation). Has received high praise.

329 W. Brueggemann. *In Man We Trust*. Atlanta: John Knox, 1972.
Explicates the Wisdom perspective, namely, that man is trusted to choose, from the material about David and Solomon. Brings this perspective to bear on the meaning of maturity and ministry.

330 J. L. Crenshaw. "In Search of Divine Presence." *RevExp* 74.3 (1977): 353–69.
Offers preliminary observations on the theology of Israel's Wisdom literature by noting diverse materials, the sages' worldview, and the thematic coherence residing in creation theology; search for order; openness to the world; and the mystery of the cosmos.

331 R. E. Clements. *Wisdom in Theology*. Grand Rapids: Eerdmans/Carlisle: Paternoster, 1992.
In a book of modest length, itself a revision of *Wisdom for a Changing World* (Berkeley: Bibal, 1990), Clements discusses Wisdom in relation to the world, health, politics, the household, and the divine realm. The book, placing Wisdom within the larger context of Israel's life, is more a prologomena to theology than a theology itself.

332 L. G. Perdue. *Wisdom and Creation: The Theology of Wisdom Literature*. Nashville: Abingdon, 1994.
Discusses the place of Wisdom in OT theology. Examines the theology of Proverbs, Job, Ecclesiastes, Ben Sira, and the Wisdom of Solomon. Stresses creation metaphors, one set related to the creation of the world, and the other set connected to the creation of humankind.

333 K. M. O'Connor. "Wisdom Literature and Experience of the Divine." Pp. 183–95 in *Biblical Theology: Problems and Perspectives* (#58).
"[E]xplores contributions of wisdom literature [via broad theological currents implicit in the text] to biblical theology by articulating some ways wisdom communicates Israel's experience of God" (p. 185). Wisdom offers a symbol of God who, for example, breaks the boundaries of gender and nationality.

7.6 Period Theologies

334 P. R. Ackroyd. *Exile and Restoration: A Study of Hebrew Thought of the Sixth Century BCE.* Philadelphia: Westminster/London: SCM, 1968.

A specialist in the field surveys the responses to the exile as represented in the Deuteronomic history, the priestly work, Ezekiel, Deutero-Isaiah, Haggai, and Zechariah.

335 T. M. Raitt. *A Theology of Exile: Judgment/Deliverance in Jeremiah and Ezekiel.* Philadelphia: Fortress, 1977.

Examines the relationship between the oracles of judgment and the oracles of salvation. Stresses the death-dealing nature of the first and the creative act of divine grace in the second. Not easy to follow.

336 R. W. Klein. *Israel in Exile: A Theological Interpretation.* Philadelphia: Fortress, 1979.

Examines several "literary works" that respond to the exile: Lamentations and exile laments, the Deuteronomistic history, and Jeremiah. All three are only cautiously hopeful in contrast to the greater optimism in Ezekiel, Second Isaiah, and the Priestly Writing in the Pentateuch. Asks for the central point around which each response to the exile turns (e.g., old promises in P; a new thing in Second Isaiah).

337 J. J. M. Roberts. "In Defence of the Monarchy: The Contribution of Israelite Kingship to Biblical Theology." Pp. 377–96 in *Ancient Israelite Religion: Essays in Honor of Frank Moore Cross.* Edited by P. D. Miller, P. D. Hanson, and S. D. McBride. Philadelphia: Fortress, 1987.

Appraises as inadequate the arguments for a negative view on royal theology (e.g., an alien institution, the conflict between human and divine kingship).

338 W. Brueggemann. "A Shattered Transcendence? Exile and Restoration." Pp. 169–82 in *Biblical Theology. Problems and Perspectives* (#58).

Examines three texts (Deut. 4:21–23; Isa. 54:7–10; Jer. 31:35–37), which place in jeopardy views on the transcendence of God. God is "radically vulnerable to the realities of Israel's life."

8

Theologies: Book by Book

Given the difficulty of formulating a theology of the OT as a whole, G. F. Hasel proposed that as an intermediate step, work should be done on individual biblical books. It has been relatively common for commentaries and dictionaries to supply summaries of a book's contents. But specific attention to the theology of a book has only more recently come to the fore. On the microlevel (a single biblical book) as well as on the macrolevel (the entire OT), the question of method immediately emerges.

Theological-type summaries of individual books are sometimes given in Introductions (cf. W. S. LaSor, D. A. Hubbard, and F. W. Bush. *Old Testament Survey: The Message, Form, and Background of the Old Testament* [Grand Rapids: Eerdmans, 1982. Second Edition: 1996]; esp. B. S. Childs. *Introduction to the Old Testament as Scripture* [Philadelphia: Fortress Press, 1979]; also R. B. Dillard and T. Longman III, *An Introduction to the Old Testament* [Grand Rapids: Zondervan, 1994]). More specialized Introductions may also carry theological summaries (cf. W. A. Van Gemeren. *Interpreting the Prophetic Word* [Grand Rapids: Zondervan, 1990]). A series, "Word Biblical Themes" by Word, in which a theological summary of sorts for a book is given through a discussion of key words or concepts is under way (e.g., *Psalms* [#377]). Volumes completed in addition to those listed below: Exodus, 1–2 Kings, Isaiah, Daniel, Hosea–Jonah.

As for commentaries, some writers in the following series offer theological summaries of individual books: New International Commentary on the Old Testament (NICOT); *Word Biblical Commentary* (*WBC*); New American Commentary (NAC); and Believers Church

Bible Commentary (BCBC). Eerdman's International Theological Commentary series, and Westminster/John Knox commentaries in the Interpretation series are intentionally theologically nuanced. Some full-fledged theologies (e.g., von Rad [#268] and Lehman [#273]; Childs, Part III [#293]) isolate single books for theological discussion.

Two recently published dictionaries carry a theological synthesis of every OT book: *Evangelical Dictionary of Biblical Theology* (#31), and *New International Dictionary of Old Testament Theology and Exegesis* (#32). See also recent encyclopedias and dictionaries listed in 1.2 (e.g., *ABD*), which sometimes summarize the theology when discussing a biblical book. In the interest of efficiency, such resources are not listed, nor is every biblical book represented in what follows.

8.1 Methodology

339 R. K. Duke. "A Model for a Theology of Biblical Historical Narratives: Proposed and Demonstrated with the Books of Chronicles." Pp. 65–77 in *History and Interpretation: Essays in Honour of John H. Hayes.* Edited by M. P. Graham, W. P. Brown, and J. K. Kuan. JSOTSup 173. Sheffield: JSOT, 1993.

The model is one of identifying the historian's values, the operative "laws of reality," attention to teleology, and the implicit ideology. A list of works on the theology of Chronicles is given on p. 74.

340 E. A. Martens. "Accessing the Theological Readings of a Biblical Book." *AUSS* 34.2 (1996): 233–49.

Distinguishes between message and theology. Illustrates from Deuteronomy the theology-shaping factors pertinent to the text (e.g., form, traditions, literary features) and factors within the theologian (e.g., imagination and creativity). Cf. R. Schultz. "Integrating Theology and Exegesis" in *NIDOTTE* (#32).

8.2 Compendia

341 W. J. Dumbrell. *The Faith of Israel: Its Expression in the Books of the Old Testament.* Grand Rapids: Baker, 1988.

Treats each book in Hebrew canonical order, summarizing its content by sections to highlight its theological purpose.

Regards the Pentateuch and the Former Prophets as theologically seminal. Disavows any single theological center.

342 R. B. Zuck (ed.). *A Biblical Theology of the Old Testament* (#51).
Each OT book, as either free-standing or as part of a larger corpus, is summarized theologically.

343 *Evangelical Dictionary of Biblical Theology* (#31).
One of the features of this work is an essay for each book of the Bible setting out the theology of that book.

344 *New International Dictionary of Old Testament Theology and Exegesis* (#32).
For each OT book there is an entry elaborating its theology. Bibliographies are sometimes quite extensive.

8.3 Books of the Old Testament

8.3.1 Genesis

345 G. W. Coats. "Strife and Reconciliation: Themes of a Biblical Theology in the Book of Genesis." *HBT* 2 (1980): 15–37.
Explores the form and content of the language of reconciliation (e.g., union of intimacy) in light of P. Stuhlmacher's proposal that "reconciliation in Christ" is a summary description of the NT.

346 V. P. Hamilton. "Theology." Pp. 38–52 in *The Book of Genesis Chapters 1–17*. NICOT. Grand Rapids: Eerdmans, 1990.
Comments theologically on promise, morality, theophany, and divine redemptive action.

8.3.2 Exodus

347 B. S. Childs. *The Book of Exodus: A Critical Theological Commentary*. Philadelphia: Westminster, 1974.
While there is not a comprehensive essay on the theology of the book, sections entitled "Theological Reflections" punctuate the commentary.

348 D. E. Gowan. *Theology in Exodus: Biblical Theology in the Form of a Commentary*. Louisville: Westminister/John Knox, 1994.
Pursues the question of how God is depicted by investigating sections (e.g., chaps. 5:1–15:21, God as destroyer).

8.3.3 Leviticus

349 J. H. Hartley. "The Message of Leviticus." Pp. lvi–lxxiii in *Leviticus. WBC*, 4. Dallas: Word, 1992.
   Discusses the following key theological themes: holiness, presence, covenant, and sacrifice.

8.3.4 Numbers

350 W. Harrelson. "Guidance in the Wilderness: The Theology of Numbers." *Int* 13 (1959): 24–36.
   Arrives at the theology utilizing the book's structure and major themes, such as murmuring.

351 R. P. Knierim. "The Book of Numbers." Pp. 155–63 in *Die Hebräische Bibel und ihre zweifache Nachgeschichte*. Festschrift für R. Rendtorff. Edited by E. Blum, C. Macholz, and E. W. Stegemann. Neukirchen-Vluyn: Neukirchener Verlag, 1990. Reprinted in *The Task of Old Testament Theology* (#57), pp. 380–88.
   On the basis of structure, genre, setting, and intention, Knierim discerns a "sanctuary camp campaign" under the leadership of Yahweh the Campaigner. The two-part structure of the book speaks to preparation for and participation in war.

8.3.5 Deuteronomy

352 R. E. Clements. *God's Chosen People: A Theological Interpretation of the Book of Deuteronomy*. Valley Forge, Pa.: Judson/ London: SCM, 1969.
   After chapters on, for example, "The Gifts of God" and "The Meaning of Worship," the final chapter deals with Deuteronomy and OT theology.

353 J. G. McConville. *Law and Theology in Deuteronomy*. JSOTSup 33. Sheffield: JSOT, 1984.
   Covenantal themes, such as "gift" and "moral order," point the way toward understanding the laws.

354 J. Goldingay. "An Evaluative Study of the Teaching of Deuteronomy." Pp. 134–66 in *Theological Diversity and the Authority of the Old Testament* (#192).

While not a full-scale theology of Deuteronomy, the chapter tests a method for dealing with the theological diversity of one book.

355 D. T. Olson. *Deuteronomy and the Death of Moses: A Theological Reading.* Minneapolis: Fortress, 1994.
Sees Deuteronomy as a catechesis dominated by two covenants, Horeb (chaps. 5–28) and Moab (chaps. 29–32), with the latter placing priority on the mercy and compassion of God.

8.3.6 Joshua

356 G. J. Wenham. "The Deuteronomic Theology of the Book of Joshua." *JBL* 90 (1971): 140–48.
The books of Deuteronomy and Joshua are bound together by five theological leitmotifs: the holy war of conquest, the distribution of land, the unity of all Israel, Joshua as the successor of Moses, and the covenant.

357 M. H. Woudstra. "Theology." Pp. 26–39 in *The Book of Joshua.* NICOT. Grand Rapids: Eerdmans, 1981.
Notes problems with method; underscores God's faithfulness and the theme of land.

358 R. D. Bell. "The Theology of Joshua." *Biblical Viewpoint* 26.2 (1992): 59–68.
Identifies seven themes (such as the Lord's presence, the Lord's gift), noting key verses in the book's seven sections (Table 3). In the eighth section (chap. 24), each theme appears twice.

8.3.7 Judges

359 J. C. Exum. "The Theological Dimension of the Samson Saga." *VT* 33 (1983): 30–45.
With the help of literary structure, explicit references to the actions of deity, and the focus given to prayer, Exum identifies the theological message: life and death at the hands of Yahweh.

9.3.8 Ruth

360 R. M. Hals. *The Theology of the Book of Ruth.* Philadelphia: Fortress, 1969.

God's providence, his all-causality in combination with his hiddenness, is the book's main theological presupposition.

361 W. S. Prinsloo. "The Theology of the Book of Ruth." *VT* 30 (1980): 330–41.

Using syntactic analysis as a control for the semantic content, Prinsloo moves from the five identifiable pericopes and their individual theological summaries to a conclusion that entails the relationship between the divine and human initiatives. Cf. R. L. Hubbard. "Theology." Pp. 66–74 in *The Book of Ruth.* NICOT. Grand Rapids: Eerdmans, 1988. Hubbard adds to the above the notion of loyalty *(ḥesed).*

8.3.9 First and Second Samuel

362 J. A. Martin. "The Theology of Samuel." *BibSac* 141/564 (1984): 303–14.

"The center of the theology of the books of Samuel hinges on this fertility principle and can be stated as follows: The well-being of the people of God (Israel) depended on their response to His choosing them as His instruments and saving them; the righteous ones, those chosen by God, prosper while those who oppose God's instruments of rulership are cut off" (p. 306).

8.3.10 First and Second Kings

363 P. R. House. "Introduction to Theological Issues." Pp. 73–82 in *The New American Commentary.* Vol. 8: *1, 2 Kings.* Nashville: Broadman & Holman, 1995.

Theological comments gravitate around ideas of monotheism versus idolatry, central worship versus high places, covenantal loyalty versus spiritual rebellion, true prophecy versus lying spirits, and God's sovereignty versus human pride.

8.3.11 First and Second Chronicles

364 R. North. "Theology of the Chronicler." *JBL* 82 (1963): 369–81.

Four themes focus the theological thought of the Chronicler: legitimacy, short-range retribution, cultus, and Davidism.

365   P. R. Ackroyd. "The Theology of the Chronicler." *Lexington Theological Quarterly* 8 (1973): 109–16.

Notes the Chronicler's technique of "patterning," and the strands within the pluriform tradition that are of theological importance: alignment with the Deuteronomist's centrality of David, temple cult, and claims to absoluteness.

366   J. Goldingay. "The Theology of the Chronicler." *BTB* 5 (1975): 99–126.

Argues that the Chronicler's theological assumptions have to do with history and eschatology; his theological emphases are worship, purity, and trusting obedience.

367   T. D. Hanks. "The Chronicler: Theologian of Grace." *EvQ* 53 (1981): 16–28.

Touches, inter alia, on the God of grace, worship as the means of grace, and the community established by grace.

368   R. B. Dillard. "Reward and Punishment in Chronicles: The Theology of Immediate Retribution." *WTJ* 46 (1984): 164–72.

Documentation for the thesis is supplied through specific announcements and the way narratives are shaped.

369   W. Johnstone. "Guilt and Atonement: The Theme of 1 and 2 Chronicles." Pp. 113–38 in *A Word in Season: Essays in Honour of William McKane*. Edited by J. D. Martin and P. R. Davies. JSOTSup 42. Sheffield: JSOT, 1986.

Notes the importance of *ma'al* (unfaithfulness) in the narrative section (1 Chron. 10) and in the genealogical section, along with some other themes.

370   S. Japhet. *The Ideology of the Book of Chronicles and Its Place in Biblical Thought*. Beiträge 3 zur Erforschung des Alten Testaments und des antiken Judentums (BEATAJ), 9. Frankfurt am Main: Peter Lang, 1989.

This is a translation of a 1973 Hebrew dissertation published in 1977. The historical account is in the service of ideology: bridging the gap between Israel's formative experience and present reality. The focus is on God, his people, each in their own right and in their interaction. God's name, retribution, election, worship, land, and kingship are important themes.

371   G. H. Jones. *1 & 2 Chronicles*. OTG. Sheffield: JSOT, 1993.

The theology (chap. 8) is organized around "God Active in History," "Israel, God's People," "The Davidic Dynasty," and "The Cult."

8.3.12 Ezra and Nehemiah

372 R. L. Braun, "Chronicles, Ezra, and Nehemiah: Theology and Literary History." Pp. 52–64 in *Studies in the Historical Books of the Old Testament*. Edited by J. A. Emerton. Supplements to Vetus Testamentum, 30. Leiden: E. J. Brill, 1979.

Compares the theology of the Chronicles with Ezra–Nehemiah in terms of retribution, Samaritans and foreigners, monarchy and temple. Concludes that the author of Chronicles was not, for the most part, the author of Ezra–Nehemiah.

373 H. G. M. Williamson. "A Theological Reading." Pp. xlviii–lii in *Ezra, Nehemiah*. WBC, 16. Waco, Tex.: Word, 1985.

Sensitive to the narrative genre, the author addresses the role of political figures in the context of divine purposes, concerns for legitimacy in the community, and orientation to Moses' Book of the Law.

8.3.13 Esther

374 M. Fox. "The Religion in the Book of Esther." *Judaism* 39 (1990): 135–47.

Discusses the absence of God in the book and the types of evidence adduced to demonstrate God's presence. The "carefully crafted indeterminacy" intends to convey uncertainty about God's role.

8.3.14 Job

375 J. E. Hartley. "The Genres and Message of the Book of Job." Pp. 37–50 in *The Book of Job*. NICOT. Grand Rapids: Eerdmans, 1988. Reprinted in *Sitting with Job*, pp. 65–78. Edited by R. B. Zuck. Grand Rapids: Baker, 1992.

Sensitive to form criticism, the author presents the message of the book using its dramatic framework and six themes, including suffering and theodicy.

8.3.15 Psalms

376 W. Brueggemann. *The Message of the Psalms: A Theological Commentary*. Augsburg Old Testament Studies. Minneapolis: Augsburg, 1984.

Categorizes the psalms under the rubrics of orientation, disorientation, and reorientation. Representative psalms in these categories are treated exegetically, usually in summary fashion. Stimulating for the scholar; useful for the pastor.

A theological approach is also found in *Israel's Praise: Doxology against Idolatry and Ideology*. Philadelphia: Fortress, 1988.

377   L. C. Allen. *Word Biblical Themes: Psalms.* Waco, Tex.: Word, 1987.

Brief chapters on key words: praise, faith, blessing, salvation, hope, Scripture. Popular in orientation.

378   H.-J. Kraus. *Theology of the Psalms.* Translated by Keith Crim. Minneapolis: Fortress, 1992. Original Title: *Theologie der Psalmen.* Neukirchen Vluyn: Neukirchener Verlag, 1979.

Regards the subject matter to be God and Israel, God and the persons in Israel, and their respective encounters. Chapter headings: God, the People of God, the Sanctuary and Its Worship, the King, the Enemy, the Individual, the Presence of God, and the Psalms and the NT. A detailed technical treatment.

379   G. T. Sheppard. "Theology and the Book of Psalms." *Int* 46 (1992): 143–55.

Concentrates on prayer as the content, lament as the form, and the shape of the book judged by the superscriptions as a way of disclosing theological insights about the meaning of conversing with God and the depiction of general humanity.

380   J. C. McCann Jr. *A Theological Introduction to the Book of Psalms: The Psalms as Torah.* Nashville: Abingdon, 1993.

Through an exegesis of selected psalms, McCann shows that the psalms not only depict who God is but especially the proper response to God. Scholarly, informed; keen on the church's appropriation of the psalms.

381   J. L. Mays. *The Lord Reigns: A Theological Handbook to the Psalms.* Louisville: Westminster/John Knox, 1994.

As a long-time student of the psalms sensitive to their use in the church as Scripture, Mays helpfully treats the psalms as prayers and praises, not through exegesis but through a theological synopsis. Many of the chapters have been previously published in journals. The book was generated in part by his commentary on the psalms (Interpretation series). Cf. his claim that "an organizing centre for the theology of the Psalms can be found in the sentence, YHWH *malak*" in "The Centre of the Psalms," pp. 231–46 in *Language, Theology, and the Bible* (#56).

8.3.16 Proverbs

382 B. K. Waltke. "The Book of Proverbs and Old Testament Theology." *BibSac* 136.544 (1979): 302–17.

Argues that the sages and the prophets were true spiritual yokefellows sharing the same Lord, cultus, faith, hope, anthropology, and epistemology. They also spoke with the same authority and made similar ethical demands. Cf. D. A. Garrett. "The Theology of Wisdom [Proverbs]." Pp. 52–59 in *The New American Commentary*. Vol. 14: *Proverbs, Ecclesiastes, Song of Songs*. Nashville: Broadman, 1993.

383 R. E. Murphy. "Proverbs and Theological Exegesis." Pp. 87–95 in *The Hermeneutical Quest: Essays in Honor of James Luther Mays*. Edited by D. G. Miller. Allison Park, Pa.: Pickwick, 1986.

Argues that the Wisdom experience, which is linked with creation and human experience, together with the theme of Lady Wisdom who provides motivation for wise conduct, represents the theological edge in Proverbs.

384 L. Boström. *The God of the Sages: The Portrayal of God in the Book of Proverbs*. Coniectanea Biblica, 29. Stockholm: Almqvist & Wiksell International, 1990.

Delineates the Lord's relationship of both nearness and remoteness to creation, world order, and retribution. Compares Proverbs with other OT and non-Israelite traditions. Well-organized and well-documented. Thorough and clear.

8.3.17 Ecclesiastes

385 J. F. Armstrong. "Ecclesiastes in Old Testament Theology." *Princeton Seminary Bulletin* 4 (1983): 16–25.

Sees the book as challenging the coherent relationship between virtue and historical fortune; the book functions as a guardian against an uncritical use of the sacred history (p. 23).

386 R. E. Murphy. "The Message of Ecclesiastes." Pp. lvi–lxix in *Ecclesiastes. WBC*, 23A. Dallas: Word, 1992.
Discusses key theological terms, for each of which specific bibliography is supplied: vanity, profit, toil, joy, portion, wisdom, fear of God, retribution, and death. Cf. his "Qoheleth and Theology." *BTB* 21 (1991): 30–33.

387 D. A. Garrett. "Theology and Purpose." Pp. 271–79 in *The New American Commentary.* Vol. 14: *Proverbs, Ecclesiastes, Song of Solomon.* Nashville: Broadman, 1993. Reprinted in *Reflecting with Solomon*, pp. 149–57. Edited by R. B. Zuck. Grand Rapids: Baker, 1994.
Assesses proposed interpretations of the book (e.g., pessimistic skeptic, preacher of joy). "Ecclesiastes *urges its readers to recognize that they are mortal.*"

8.3.18 Song of Songs

388 D. A. Garrett. "Theology of Song of Songs." Pp. 375–80 in *The New American Commentary.* Vol. 14: *Proverbs, Ecclesiastes, Song of Songs.* Nashville: Broadman, 1993.
Responds positively to Karl Barth's view that the Song of Songs portrays the persistence of grace in spite of all sin. Sexuality is a good thing, protected by marriage.

389 O. Keel. "The Song of Songs and Yahwism." Pp. 30–37 in *The Song of Songs.* Translated by F. J. Gaiser. Minneapolis: Fortress, 1994. Original Title: *Das Hohelied.* Zurich: Theologischer Verlag.
Underscores love, which has "little to do with morality and theology" as an elemental power.

8.3.19 Isaiah

390 T. C. Vriezen. "Essentials of the Theology of Isaiah." Pp. 128–46 in *Israel's Prophetic Heritage.* Edited by B. W. Anderson and W. Harrelson. New York: Harper & Brothers, 1962.
Essential concepts include God's holiness, guilt, judgment, and the demand for faith. Isaiah emphasizes God's design for

the world and God's "wonderfulness." Cf. pp. liv–lvii in
J. D. W. Watts. *Isaiah 1–33. WBC*, 24. Waco, Tex.: Word, 1985.
Watts describes the theology in terms of Yahweh's strategy
with Israel and Jerusalem.

391 G. F. Hasel. *The Remnant: The History and Theology of the Remnant Idea from Genesis to Isaiah.* Andrews University Monographs, 5. Berrien Springs, Mich.: Andrews University Press, 1972.
A revised version of a doctoral dissertation. Sees the remnant idea as a central element in the theology of Isaiah.

392 R. W. Klein. "Going Home—A Theology of Second Isaiah." *CurTM* 5 (1978): 198–210.
The message about homegoing is entailed in the theological context of God's credentials, Cyrus the Messiah, abundant forgiveness, God's promises, the new exodus, God and the nations, and Israel's vocation. For Isaiah 40–66, see pp. 299–328 in Lehman (#273). Cf. E. Achtemeier. *The Community and Message of Isaiah 56–66: A Theological Commentary.* Minneapolis: Augsburg, 1982.

393 C. Stuhlmüller. "Deutero-Isaiah (chaps. 40–55): Major Transitions in the Prophet's Theology and Contemporary Scholarship." *CBQ* 42 (1980): 1–29.
A table clearly displays the topics—Yahweh, Israel, Zion-Jerusalem, the nations, and the Servant—each with subtopics and references. The author proceeds according to the sections, chapters 41–48, chapters 49–55, the Servant Songs, and chapter 40 (overture).

394 J. J. M. Roberts. "Isaiah in Old Testament Theology." *Int* 36.2 (1982): 130–43. Reprinted in *Interpreting the Prophets,* pp. 62–74. Edited by J. L. Mays and P. J. Achtemeier. Philadelphia: Fortress, 1987.
The central core of Isaianic theology is the vision of Yahweh as the Holy One of Israel. Developments and implications are noted for First Isaiah, Second Isaiah, Third Isaiah, and Other Isaiahs.

395 J. N. Oswalt. "Theology." Pp. 31–44 in *The Book of Isaiah Chapters 1–39.* NICOT. Grand Rapids: Eerdmans, 1986.
Organizes the thought of Isaiah according to the following rubrics: God, humanity and the world, sin and redemption.

8.3.20 Jeremiah

396 T. W. Overholt. *The Threat of Falsehood: A Study in the Theology of the Book of Jeremiah.* STB², 16. London: SCM, 1970.
Centers on the term *šeqer*, deception as falsehood, as applied to a sense of security, prophetic opponents, and idolatry.

397 R. E. Manahan. "A Theology of Pseudoprophets: A Study in Jeremiah." *Grace Theological Journal* 1 (1980): 77–96.
Adopting methods that include audience response, Manahan concludes that pseudoprophets held to a "para-covenantal" theology, with hopes attached to temple and dynasty.

398 J. A. Thompson. "The Message of Jeremiah." Pp. 107–17 in *The Book of Jeremiah.* NICOT. Grand Rapids: Eerdmans, 1980.
Topics treated are God, Israel the nation and individual, sin and repentance, and the future hope.

8.3.21 Lamentations

399 N. K. Gottwald. *Studies in the Book of Lamentations.* SBT. Chicago: Allenson, 1954.
Gottwald finds "the situational key to the theology of Lamentations in the tension between Deuteronomic faith and historical adversity" (pp. 52–53) rather than in the doctrine of retribution and reward. Two additional chapters discuss doom and hope.

400 B. Albrektson. *Studies in the Text and Theology of the Book of Lamentations.* Lund: Gleerup, 1963.
Reviews Gottwald's position, but holds that more decisive is the tension between the traditions of Zion's inviolability and the actual brute facts.

401 R. B. Salters. *Jonah & Lamentations.* OTG. Sheffield: JSOT, 1994.
In a chapter devoted to the theology of Lamentations, Salters underlines notions of sin, the work of Yahweh, and hope.

402 C. Westermann. "The Theological Significance of Lamentations." Pp. 221–35 in *Lamentations: Issues and Interpretation.* Translated by C. Muenchow. Minneapolis: Fortress, 1994.
The departure point is the lament. Gravitates around Yahweh as "Lord of History," the theological significance of

chapter 3, and the importance of Lamentations for a biblical theology today.

8.3.22 Ezekiel

403 A. Luc. "A Theology of Ezekiel: God's Name and Israel's History." *JETS* 26.2 (1983): 137–43.
Collates the subject of God's name and Israel's past, her present crisis, and her future restoration.

404 H. McKeating. *Ezekiel.* OTG. Sheffield: JSOT, 1993.
Identifies theologically the redrawing of history, remnant, sin, and expiation—all within the context of judgment and hope.

8.3.22 Daniel

405 A. J. Ferch. "Authorship, Theology, and Purpose of Daniel." Pp. 3–83 in *Symposium on Daniel: Introductory and Exegetical Studies.* Edited by F. B. Holbrook. Daniel and Revelation Committee series 2. Washington, D.C.: Biblical Research Institute, General Conference of Seventh-day Adventists, 1986.
God is the eternal Ruler of the world. Human pride is contrasted with human dependence on God. Cf. E. H. Merrill. "Daniel as a Contribution to Kingdom Theology." Pp. 211–25 in *Essays in Honor of J. Dwight Pentecost.* Edited by S. D. Toussaint and C. H. Dyer. Chicago: Moody, 1986.

8.3.23 Hosea

406 W. Eichrodt. "The Holy One in Your Midst: The Theology of Hosea." Translated by L. Gaston. *Int* 15 (1961): 259–73.
"The holy God exalted in his majesty above all human thoughts, who nevertheless strives in judgment and grace for the turning of his people to his saving love: this is the real content of the theology of Hosea."

407 R. L. Smith. "Major Motifs of Hosea." *SWJT* 18 (1975): 22–32.
Covers the topics of harloty, love, the knowledge of God, wickedness, judgment, and hope.

408 D. B. Wyrtzen. "The Theological Center of the Book of Hosea." *BibSac* 141 (1984): 315–29.

Hosea presents "*an intensely personal divine restorative con-frontation* with Israel." By one who completed a Th.D. dissertation on "A Biblical Theology of Hosea" at Dallas Theological Seminary, 1980.

8.3.24 Joel

409 W. S. Prinsloo. *The Theology of the Book of Joel.* BZAW, 163. Berlin: Walter de Gruyter, 1985.

Examines what the book of Joel "tells us about Yahweh" through attention to each pericope (given in transcription from the Hebrew). A summary is given in chapter 11 (pp. 122–27): Joel is a *theocentric book* with Yahweh as the main character.

8.3.25 Amos

410 C. G. Howie. "Expressly for Our Time: The Theology of Amos." *Int* 13 (1959): 273–85.

The topic is discussed under the following divisions: (1) Yahweh is God alone; (2) the media of divine revelation; (3) worship and the common life; (4) the nature of election; and (5) the essence of sin.

411 R. L. Smith. "The Theological Implications of the Prophecy of Amos." *SWJT* (1966): 49–56.

Discerns the theology from Amos's presuppositions having to do with what God did (election, covenant, deliverance), what nations and Israel did (transgress), and what God was about to do (judge, but also restore).

412 D. L. Williams. "The Theology of Amos." *RevExp* 63 (1966): 393–403.

The message of Amos "is primarily a re-presentation of the Mosaic faith." The theology turns around cult, the Day of Yahweh, judgment, and hope.

413 G. V. Smith. "Theological Themes." Pp. 9–14 in *Amos: A Commentary.* Grand Rapids: Zondervan, 1989.

Holds that "the theology of a book is rooted in syntactical and semantic indicators." Gives attention primarily to the names and description of Yahweh and classifies the kinds of activity attributed to God (e.g., revealing, judging). Cf. D. W. Bailey.

"Theological Themes in the Prophecy of Amos." *The Theological Educator* 52 (1995): 79–85.

8.3.26 Jonah

414 T. E. Fretheim. "Jonah and Theodicy." *ZAW* 90 (1978): 227–37.
Holds that the conclusions drawn from 4:10f., namely, that the movement is from creation to universal compassion, are flawed; instead, the movement is from creation to the rights of a sovereign God.

415 R. B. Salters. *Jonah & Lamentations* (#401).
Finds the purpose/theology, after reviewing earlier proposals, to be in Jonah 4: God's mercy and freedom to change his mind.

8.3.26 Micah

416 J. L. Mays. "The Theological Purpose of the Book of Micah." Pp. 276–87 in *Beiträge zur alttestamentlichen Theologie* (#47).
Describes a unity of intention discernible in the arrangement of material in the final form of the book. Compares the two major parts (1:2–5:15; 6:1–7:20). The linearization of the units portrays, for example, Yahweh's judgment and salvation.

8.3.27 Nahum/Habakkuk/Zephaniah

417 O. P. Robertson. *The Books of Nahum, Habakkuk, and Zephaniah.* NICOT. Grand Rapids: Eerdmans, 1990.
Messianism in the three books is limited; the message of the three prophets is theocentric and revolves around subjects such as the justice and judgment of God, the covenant of God, and the salvation of God.

8.3.28 Micah–Malachi

418 R. L. Smith. "The Shape of Theology in the Book of Malachi." *SWJT* 30.1 (1987): 22–27.
Malachi was concerned about covenant, cult, ethical conduct, and the future. Though these themes are related, Malachi does not specify the precise nature of that relationship.

419 R. L. Smith. *Micah–Malachi.* Word Biblical Themes. Dallas, Tex.:
Word, 1990.

A long-term professor at Southwestern Baptist Theological
Seminary selects pertinent theological themes for each of the
last seven books of the OT and treats these in succinct fashion. Popular in approach. Readily adapted for sermons.

$\mathcal{9}$

Monographs on Selected
Biblical Themes

OT theology integrates biblical themes and motifs. A selection of
themes and monographs (rather than articles) treating these themes
follows. Since books for each subject are numerous, only a few relevant titles have been selected. Recent works or those with further bibliography have been favored.

Sources for additional entries include *IZBG* (#2), *Elenchus of Biblica* (#6), and *The Old Testament: A Bibliography* (#8). A helpful bibliography (primarily of German works) on selected themes is found in
JBTh 1 (1986) (#37). See also the Word Biblical Themes series (e.g.,
#377).

9.1 Anger

420 B. E. Baloian. *Anger in the Old Testament.* American University
Studies: Series VII, Theology and Religion 99. New York/San
Francisco/Bern: Lang, 1992.
Seeks, inter alia, the theological viewpoint the texts contain
about both human and divine anger. Divine anger is subordi-
nated to goals of justice and love.

9.2 Anthropology

421 W. Eichrodt. *Man in the Old Testament.* Studies in Biblical
Theology, 4. Translated by K. and R. Gregor Smith. London: SCM,

1951. Original Title: *Das Menschenverständnis des alten Testaments*. Zürich: Zwingli-Verlag, n.d.

A small booklet stressing unconditional obligation and belief in the Creator as decisive for OT anthropology. Not easy reading.

422 H. W. Wolff. *An Anthropology of the Old Testament*. Translated by Margaret Kohl. Philadelphia: Fortress/London: SCM, 1974. Original Title: *Anthropologie des Alten Testaments*. Munich: Chr. Kaiser Verlag, 1973.

A reference-type book that has worn well. Sample chapters: The Being of Man (e.g., reasonable man), The Time of Man (e.g., life and death), and The World of Man (e.g., individual and community). Word studies of the Hebrew, such as *nephesh, basar,* and *ruach,* are a welcome feature.

423 S. Terrien. *Till the Heart Sings: A Biblical Theology of Manhood and Womanhood*. Philadelphia: Fortress, 1985.

Argues from Genesis and Wisdom literature (e.g., Song of Songs) that the main thrust of the Hebrew Bible and the NT does not favor the male sex but speaks of sexual mutuality. Includes a chapter on the gender of God. The last part of the book is devoted to the NT and the developing church. No footnotes, but an extensive select bibliography.

9.3 Apocalyptic (See also §9.9)

424 W. Dumbrell. *The End of the Beginning: Rev. 21–23 and the Old Testament*. Grand Rapids: Baker, 1985.

Identifies five themes: the new Jerusalem, the new temple, the new covenant, the new Israel, and the new creation, and traces these through the Bible.

425 P. D. Hanson. "Biblical Apocalypticism: The Theological Dimension." *HBT* 7.2 (1985): 1–20.

Theologically apocalypticism offers a universal perspective, transcends parochialism, and searches for cosmic harmony. For the community of faith, apocalypticism addresses social, political, and possible nuclear chaos.

9.4 Blessing

426   H.-P. Müller. "Segen im Alten Testament." *ZTK* 87 (1990): 1–32. Half the article deals with the semantic word field of blessing (e.g., curse) and the function of deity and humans in blessing; the second half notes blessing as a religious phenomenon and addresses its theological significance. Cf. Westermann (#289, #465), and also his *Blessing in the Bible and the Life of the Church*. Translated by Keith Crim. Philadelphia: Fortress, 1978. Original Title: *Der Segen in der Bibel und im Handeln der Kirche*. Muenchen: Chr. Kaiser Verlag, 1968.

9.5 Covenant

427   D. J. McCarthy. *The Old Testament Covenant: A Survey of Current Opinions*. Growing Points in Theology. Richmond: John Knox/Oxford: Basil Blackwood, 1972. Original Title: *Der Gottesbund im Alten Testament*. SBS. Stuttgart: Verlag Katholisches Bibelwerk GmbH, 1967.
  Discusses covenant under topics of semantics, treaty, prophets and kingship, and theology (pp. 4–5, 53–56, 86–89). Extensive bibliography.

428   J. Bright. *Covenant and Promise: The Prophetic Understanding of the Future in Pre-exilic Israel*. Philadelphia: Westminster, 1976.
  Concludes, after an examination particularly of Jeremiah, that two visions of the future collided in sixth-century Judah. One vision, centering in the Davidic covenant (divine election, promises), led to optimism; another vision, shaped by the Sinai covenant (righteous requirements), made for a darker outlook.

429   W. Vogels. *God's Universal Covenant: A Biblical Study*. Ottawa: University of Ottawa Press, 1979.
  A study of mostly OT texts beginning with J and P texts and moving through the historical and prophetic material to establish the position that "covenant" and "universalism" are notions that belong together.

430   O. P. Robertson. *The Christ of the Covenants*. Grand Rapids: Baker, 1980.

Ties the themes from the various covenants (Adam, Noah, Abraham, Mosaic, Davidic) to Jesus Christ. Defines covenant as a bond in blood sovereignly administered.

431 W. J. Dumbrell. *Covenant and Creation: An Old Testament Covenantal Theology.* Exeter: Paternoster/New South Wales: Lancer, 1984. South Africa Edition: Capetown: Oxford University Press. Paperback Edition: Grand Rapids: Baker, 1993.

Exegetical and theological explorations of the covenants with Noah (creation), Abraham, Sinai, David, and the New Covenant in order to present an overall theological approach to the OT.

432 A. S. Kapelrud. "The Prophets and Covenant." Pp. 175–83 in *In the Shelter of Elyon: Essays on Ancient Palestinian Life and Literature in Honor of G. W. Ahlström.* Edited by W. B. Barrick and J. R. Spencer. JSOTSup 31. Sheffield: JSOT, 1984.

Holds that covenant "was alive at an early period in Israel" (p. 180). Prophets were mute on the subject so as not to evoke ideas of protection by a national God. Interacts with views of the Uppsala school (e.g., I. Engnell); L. Perlitt, who holds that covenant is late (*Bundestheologie im Alten Testament,* WMANT 36 [Neukirchen-Vluyn: Neukirchener Verlag, 1969]); and E. Kutsch (*Verheissung und Gesetz: Untersuchungen zum sogenannten 'Bund' in Alten Testament,* BZAW 131 [Berlin: Walter de Gruyter, 1972]).

433 T. E. McComiskey. *The Covenants of Promise: A Theology of the Old Testament Covenants.* Grand Rapids: Baker/Nottingham: InterVarsity, 1985.

Proposes a bicovenantal structure in which a primary promissory category (notably in the Abrahamic covenant) is qualified by an administrative set of elements.

434 E. W. Nicholson. *God and His People: Covenant Theology in the Old Testament.* Oxford: Clarendon, 1986. Paperback Edition: 1988.

Surveys the debate around covenant since Wellhausen, noting M. Noth, E. Kutsch, L. Perlitt, and M. Weber. Examines pre-Deuteronomic texts (e.g., Hosea), but holds with Perlitt that the Deuteronomic movement developed a fully elaborated theology of covenant. For a quite different approach to the larger topic, see R. L. Hubbard Jr. et al. (eds.), *Studies in Old Testament Theology* (#53).

435 R. Murray. *The Cosmic Covenant: Biblical Themes of Justice, Peace and the Integrity of Creation.* Heythrop Monographs, 7. London: Sheed & Ward, 1992.

Critiques the preoccupation with the historical significance of covenant. The religious worldview entailed in covenant includes the themes of creation and order, themes Murray traces into patristic and talmudic thinking.

436 N. Lohfink. "Der Begriff 'Bund' in der biblischen Theologie." Pp. 19–36 in *Der Gott Israels und die Völker: Untersuchungen zum Jesajabuch und zu den Psalmen,* by N. Lohfink and E. Zenger. SBS, 154. Stuttgart: KWB, 1994.

First a summary of the research is given; in a second section a synthetic sketch is given of the "canonical theology of covenant" in which the relationship between covenant and other themes, such as law, are noted.

437 J. H. Walton. *Covenant: God's Purpose, God's Plan.* Grand Rapids: Zondervan, 1994.

Sees the purpose of covenant to be primarily a mechanism for God's self-revelation, and so superseding other goals, including bondedness, redemption, and promise. Suggestive but not fully compelling.

438 R. Rendtorff. *Die "Bundesformel": Eine exegetisch-theologische Untersuchung.* SBS, 160. Stuttgart: Katholisches Bibelwerk, 1995.

Different versions of the formula "I will be your God, and you will be my people" are examined as they occur in the Pentateuch, Deuteronomy, Samuel–Kings, Jeremiah, and Ezekiel. The formula may help bridge diverse theological concepts.

9.6 Creation

439 G. von Rad. "The Theological Problem of the Old Testament Doctrine of Creation." Pp. 131–43 in *The Problem of the Hexateuch and Other Essays.* Translated by E. W. Trueman Dicken. New York: McGraw-Hill/Edinburgh: Oliver & Boyd, 1966. Reprinted in B. W. Anderson, *Creation in the Old Testament,* pp. 53–64. German essay of 1936 reprinted in *Gesammelte Studien zum Alten Testament.* Munich: Chr. Kaiser Verlag, 1958.

This frequently referenced essay addresses the relationship of creation to redemption and concludes that the doctrine of creation was not an independent Christian doctrine but subordinate to soteriological considerations.

440 B. W. Anderson. *Creation versus Chaos: The Reinterpretation of Mythical Symbolism in the Bible.* New York: Association Press, 1967. Reprinted: Philadelphia: Fortress, 1987.

By a long-time student of the creation theme. The reinterpretation entails creation subsumed under a historical intention. Creation faith is doxological, that is, it offers an alternative world in which to live and work. See also *Creation in the Old Testament* (Fortress, 1984), which he edited, and his fourteen collected essays, some now revised, published between 1955 and 1994 in his *From Creation to New Creation: Old Testament Perspectives.* OBT. Minneapolis: Fortress, 1994.

441 W. H. Bellinger Jr. "Maker of Heaven and Earth: The Old Testament and Creation Theology." *SWJT* 32.2 (1990): 27–35.

Notes the challenge to von Rad (cf. #268) by H. H. Schmidt ("Creation, Righteousness and Salvation: 'Creation Theology' as the Broad Horizon of Biblical Theology." Pp. 102–17 in B. W. Anderson, *Creation in the Old Testament*) and R. P. Knierim ("Cosmos and History in Israel's Theology." *HBT* 3 [1981]: 59–123). Citing the psalms and Wisdom literature, Bellinger concludes that the OT can no longer be described predominantly as "salvation history."

442 R. Rentdorff. "Some Reflections on Creation as a Topic of Old Testament Theology." Pp. 204–12 in *Priests, Prophets and Scribes: Essays on Formation and Heritage of Second Temple Judaism in Honour of Joseph Blenkinsopp.* Edited by E. Ulrich et al. JSOTSup 149. Sheffield: JSOT, 1992.

Proposes creation as the starting point of OT theology. Reads creation texts—Genesis, Deuteronomy, Nehemiah 9:6–37/ Psalm 136—from a canonical perspective.

443 J. R. Middleton. "Is Creation Theology Inherently Conservative? A Dialogue with Walter Brueggemann." *HTR* 87 (1994): 257–77.

Brueggemann is said to view creation negatively because it functioned in the Abraham-David-Royal Zion traditions as "structure legitimation" and so could be used oppressively. Middleton notes liberation creation themes in Genesis and Exodus. Brueggemann responds (pp. 279–89), noting the impulses that charted his assessment and citing new developments in creation theology.

444 B. Och. "Creation and Redemption: Towards a Theology of Creation." *Judaism* 44.2 (1995): 226–43.

Och's purpose is "to correct the injustice done to the doctrine of creation and reassert its centrality in Biblical theology and interpretation." Sees redemption via Abraham and Exodus/Sinai as the implementation of creation.

9.7 Cult/Worship

445 Y. Hattori. "Theology of Worship in the Old Testament." Pp. 21–50 in *Worship: Adoration and Action.* Edited by D. A. Carson. Grand Rapids: Published on behalf of the World Evangelical Fellowship by Baker and Paternoster, 1993.

Identifies basic worship elements in the history of Israel discussed by periods. Although clearly a survey, the 139 footnotes list wide-ranging resources.

446 R. D. Nelson. *Raising Up a Faithful Priest: Community and Priesthood in Biblical Theology.* Louisville: Westminster/John Knox, 1993.

"Intended to be an introduction to what can be said theologically about priests on the basis of the biblical text and the priestly role in Israelite religion and society." Employs insights from anthropology; a good chapter on "Priesthood and Theology." One chapter deals with the NT (Hebrews; 1 Peter). Five pages of suggestions for further reading.

9.8 Death/Resurrection

447 G. T. Milazzo. *The Protest and the Silence: Suffering, Death and Biblical Theology.* Minneapolis: Fortress, 1992.

Notes the inadequacies of the Biblical Theology Movement. Interacts with the psalms and Balentine's interpretation of lament, with apocalyptic literature and with Wisdom (Job, Ecclesiastes), and points in the end to a protest theism.

448 B. C. Ollenburger. "If Mortals Die, Will They Live Again? The Old Testament and Resurrection." *Ex Auditu* 9 (1993): 29–44.

The hope that God the Creator will keep solidarity with the
dead is found in Isaiah, Job, and Psalms. The promise of resurrection, found in Daniel and 2 Maccabees, serves as motivation for faithfulness to God.

9.9 Eschatology (See also §9.3)

449 T. C. Vriezen. "Prophecy and Eschatology." Pp. 199–229 in *Congress Volume: Copenhagen 1953*. Supplements to VT 1. Edited
by G. W. Anderson et al. Leiden: Brill, 1953.
Judgment and salvation motifs are identified chiefly around
two culminating points: Isaiah (surrounded by Amos, Hosea,
and Micah) and Deutero-Isaiah.

450 O. Plöger. *Theocracy and Eschatology*. Translated by S. Rudman.
Orginal Title: *Theokratie und Eschatologie*. Neukirchen: Krers
Moers, 1959. Second Edition: 1962. Oxford: Blackwell, 1968.
Distinguishes four periods of eschatological ideas (e.g., the
fourth is a dualistic eschatology). "Eschatology is not a wish
dream that admits of a psychological explanation, but a religious certainty which springs immediately from the Israelite
faith in God as rooted in the history of its salvation." A benchmark essay.

451 W. Zimmerli. *Man and His Hope in the Old Testament*. SBT[2].
London: SCM, 1971. Original Title: *Der Mensch und seine Hoff-
nung im Alten Testament*. Göttingen: Vandenhoeck und
Ruprecht, 1968.
A collection of ten lectures examining hope in various literary strata (e.g., Wisdom, Psalms, the Yahwistic writings,
Deuteronomistic history, prophetic writings, apocalyptic). The
final chapter, "Conversation with Ernst Bloch," indicates the
occasion for the book.

452 H. D. Preuss (ed.). *Eschatologie im Alten Testament*. Wege der
Forschung 480. Darmstadt: Wissenschaftliche Buchgesellschaft,
1978.
The editor surveys previous studies, differing definitions of
eschatology, and views of the origin and development of eschatology. Twenty-three articles from journals (1951–74) follow.

453 D. E. Gowan. *Eschatology in the Old Testament*. Philadelphia:
Fortress/Edinburgh: T. & T. Clark, 1986, 1987.

Zion is central in Israel's hope for the future transformation of society, the individual, and nature. Emphasizes traditions rather than contributions of individual authors.

9.10 Ethics

454 J. Muilenburg. *The Way of Israel: Biblical Faith and Ethics*. Religious Perspectives, 5. New York: Harper & Brothers, 1961. First Paperback Edition: 1965.
A "way" (conduct, behavior) is delineated in Scripture for modern people to follow. In easy-to-read prose, a gifted scholar charts the course by discussing the symbols of the way, the way of leaders (lawgivers, prophets, the wise), the way of worship, and the way of the future. Stresses the uniqueness of Israel's faith. A pithy book.

455 W. C. Kaiser Jr. *Toward Old Testament Ethics*. Grand Rapids: Zondervan, 1983.
Treats definition and method; summarizes moral texts (e.g., Decalogue, Deuteronomy) and elaborates the content of ethics around the key term "holiness." The approach is to stress principles. Parts IV and V deal with moral difficulties and NT applications.

456 C. J. H. Wright. *An Eye for an Eye*. Downers Grove: InterVarsity, 1983. British Edition: *Living as the People of God*. Leicester: InterVarsity, 1983.
The OT areas of Law, Wisdom, and prophecy are taken into account, largely as paradigms rather than as universally applicable principles. Scholarly and informed, but understandable by the general reader. Based on a revision of a doctoral dissertation that has since been published as *God's People in God's Land: Family, Land and Property in the Old Testament*. Grand Rapids: Eerdmans/Exeter: Paternoster, 1990.

457 B. C. Birch. *Let Justice Roll Down: The Old Testament, Ethics and the Christian Life*. Louisville: Westminster/John Knox, 1991.
Uses the genre of narrative, the flow of Israel's story from creation to exile, plus Wisdom to present ethical dimensions. Little tie-in with the NT, but makes application to current life. Subject, author, Scripture, and Hebrew word indexes. Cf. his article, "Moral Agency, Community, and the Character of God

in the Hebrew Bible," as well as other articles (e.g., J. W. Barton, "The Basis of Ethics in the Hebrew Bible") in *Semeia* 66 (1994), an issue devoted to ethics.

458 W. Janzen. *Old Testament Ethics: A Paradigmatic Approach.* Louisville: Westminster/John Knox, 1994.

Identifies several model stories that function as paradigms for ethics, with the familial paradigm being given a privileged position. Other paradigms, each connected with Jesus, are the priestly (holy life), Wisdom, royal (just life), and prophetic (serving/suffering). A fresh and stimulating approach. Well-indexed.

459 C. J. H. Wright. "The Ethical Authority of the Old Testament: A Survey of Approaches. Part I." *TynBul* 43 (1992): 101–20. "Part II." *Tyn Bul* 43 (1992): 203–31.

In Part I Wright deals with the views taken toward OT laws in the early church, the Reformation, and, more recently, by Protestants. Part II singles out exegetical approaches as represented by W. Kaiser, J. Goldingay, dispensationalists, and theonomists; Wright presents his own method.

460 E. Otto. *Theologische Ethik des Alten Testaments.* Theologische Wissenschaaft 3/2 Stuttgart: Verlag W. Kohlhammer, 1994.

Treats the Book of the Covenant, Wisdom, the contributions of Deuteronomy and P, and so on, grounding ethics in God's revelation and history. Excellent bibliography for each section. Described as "breathtaking in its approach and depth" and as "an essential reference work."

9.11 Faith (See §9.13)

9.12 God/Yahweh

Several articles in *JBTh* 2 (1987) discuss the subject, "The One God"; others treat the God of the two Testaments.

461 C. J. Labuschagne. *The Incomparability of Yahweh in the Old Testament.* Pretoria Oriental Series, 5. Leiden: E. J. Brill, 1966.

Identifies expressions (e.g., "Who is like . . .") denoting incomparability and examines the content of such claims. Examines other ANE religions. Concludes that Israel's statements of incomparability are rooted in the exodus, and show the bearing of the research on biblical theology. A well-researched work.

462 J. S. Chesnut. *The Old Testament Understanding of God.* Philadelphia: Westminster, 1968.

Explores for the general reader "the most significant expressions of ancient Israel's understanding of God" (e.g., God of Moses, The Lord of Hosts, God of the Prophets, God of the Covenant) with an emphasis on the fact of God's existence.

463 G. H. Parke-Taylor. *Yahweh: The Divine Name in the Bible.* Waterloo, Ont.: Wilfrid Laurier University Press, 1975.

Largely semantic and historical; theological implications are treated in chapter 5 (pp. 63–78).

464 P. Trible. *God and the Rhetoric of Sexuality.* OBT. Philadelphia: Fortress, 1978.

Accents "neglected themes," such as female imagery for God, through careful exegetical study of texts about "the image of God" (Gen. 2–3), metaphors about womb-like compassion (Jeremiah), and related material in Ruth and Song of Songs.

465 C. Westermann. *What Does the Old Testament Say about God?* Edited by F. W. Golka. Atlanta: John Knox, 1979.

By a German Lutheran. Based on the Sprunt Lectures at Union Theological Seminary–Virginia. Discusses the "Saving God and History," "The Blessing God and Creation," "Judgment/Mercy," and "The Old Testament and Jesus Christ."

466 D. Patrick. *The Rendering of God in the Old Testament.* OBT. Philadelphia: Fortress, 1981.

Works from an artistic rather than a historical perspective. Depicts God as a *dramatis persona* within a story, so that from speech and incidents God's identity emerges and his role becomes clarified.

467 W. Zimmerli. *I Am Yahweh.* Translated by D. W. Stott. Edited by and Introduction by W. Brueggemann. Atlanta: John Knox, 1982.

Three essays, "I Am Yahweh," "Knowledge of God according to the Book of Ezekiel," and "The Word of Divine Self-Manifestation (Proof-saying): A Prophetic Genre," are especially basic to Zimmerli's entire theological program.

468 T. E. Fretheim. *The Suffering of God: An Old Testament Perspective.* OBT. Philadelphia: Fortress, 1984.

Focuses on images and metaphors that modify the conventional understanding of God as vindictive and punitive. Analyzes God–world relationships and shows that God suffers because, with, and for the world and its peoples.

469 T. N. D. Mettinger. *In Search of God: The Meaning and Message of the Everlasting Names.* Translated by F. H. Cryer. Philadelphia: Fortress, 1988. Original Title: *Gudsbeteckningar och gudsbild i Gamla Testamentet.* Bokförlaget Libris Örebro, 1987.
Treatment of divine titles and designations: I Am, God of the Fathers, the Living God, The Lord as King, The Lord of Hosts, and God as "Redeemer," "Savior," and "Creator."

9.13 Grace/Faith/Faithfulness

470 R. M. Hals. *Grace and Faith in the Old Testament.* Minneapolis: Augsburg, 1980.
A booklet in popular style noting how God's grace surfaces in his actions, choices, laws, judgments, and promises.

471 K. D. Sakenfeld. *Faithfulness in Action: Loyalty in Biblical Perspective.* OBT. Philadelphia: Fortress, 1985.
Extends her discussion of faithfulness (help in need, an attitude demonstrated to someone in need by a person with an ability to help) beyond her initial book, *The Meaning of Hesed in the Hebrew Bible* (Missoula: Scholars, 1976), by way of stories, a discussion of God's loyalty, and observations about the import of these understandings for contemporary lifestyles. For a penetrating analysis of *ḥesed* but somewhat differently nuanced, cf. F. I. Andersen, "Yahweh, the Kind and Sensitive God." Pp. 41–88 in *God Who Is Rich in Mercy: Essays Presented to Dr. D. B. Knox.* Edited by P. T. O'Brien and D. G. Peterson. Homebush West, NSW: Anzea, 1986.

9.14 Healing/Health

472 M. L. Brown. *Israel's Divine Healer.* SOTBT. Grand Rapids: Zondervan, 1995.
A full-scale treatment—philological, exegetical, historical, and theological—on healing in the OT. One chapter (30 pp.) is devoted to the NT.

9.15 Justice/Righteousness/Holiness

473 N. H. Snaith. *The Distinctive Ideas of the Old Testament.* New York: Schocken, 1964. Second Printing: 1969. London: Epworth, 1944. Reprinted: 1969, 1983.

The distinctive elements are held to be the holiness of God, the righteousness of God, the salvation of God, the covenant-love of God, the election-love of God, and the Spirit of God. A book that is something of a benchmark.

474 J. Kräsovec, *La justice (ṣdq) de Dieu dans la Bible hébraique et l'interprétation juive et chrétienne.* Orbis Biblicus et Orientalis, 76. Göttingen: Vandenhoeck und Ruprecht, 1988.

An extensive study (452 pp.) on divine (not human) justice. Deals with 140 of the 523 occurrences of the Hebrew root ṣdq. The central part deals also with Jewish and Christian interpretations up to the Reformers. The final section discusses the semantic field of the root term and concludes that God's justice has to do essentially with a personal salvific relationship with his people. Holds, contrary to some, that ṣdq does not indicate a "norm."

475 J. G. Gammie. *Holiness in Israel.* OBT. Minneapolis: Fortress, 1989.

Describes different understandings of holiness (= cleanness) as found in priestly (ritual purity), prophetic (purity of social justice), and Wisdom (cleanness of individual morality) literature.

476 H. G. Reventlow and Y. Hoffman (eds.). *Justice and Righteousness: Biblical Themes and Their Influence.* FS B. Uffenheimer. JSOTSup 137. Sheffield: JSOT, 1992.

An assortment of fifteen essays, mostly by Jewish and German scholars. Those of a theological cast discuss land and justice, theodicy in the book of Qohelet, law and ethics in the Hebrew Bible, the creativity of theodicy, righteousness as order of the world, theodicy and ethics in the prophecy of Ezekiel, justice and righteousness.

9.16 Kingdom of God/Kingship

477 J. Gray. *The Biblical Doctrine of the Reign of God.* Edinburgh: T. & T. Clark, 1979.

Interacts with the issues centered on the Enthronement
Psalms but extends the investigation to pre- and postexilic
prophets and prophetic eschatology, the ideal kingship of the
Messiah, and the NT. Many valuable Hebrew linguistic prob-
ings (e.g., *šub šebut* as "rehabilitation").

478 B. C. Ollenburger. *Zion the City of the Great King: A Theological Symbol of the Jerusalem Cult.* JSOTSup 41. Sheffield: JSOT,
1987.
A focused study of texts in Psalms and Isaiah. Zion as a theological symbol denotes security grounded in Yahweh as creator and as royal defender of a world order.

479 M. J. Selman. "The Kingdom of God in the Old Testament."
TynBul 40 (1989): 161–83.
Selman focuses on Daniel and Chronicles, both of whom drew
on the prophets and particularly on the Psalms (e.g., 45, 145).
Two different manifestations emerge: (1) a universal and cos-
mic reign, and (2) a Zion-centered reign in Israel.

480 M. Z. Brettler. *God Is King: Understanding an Israelite Metaphor.* JSOTSup 76. Sheffield: JSOT, 1989.
The psalmic expression "God is King" does not refer to Israel's
recognition made within the cult, but celebrates God as so
recognized by the nations. Extensive and helpful bibliography.

9.17 Land

481 W. Brueggemann. *The Land: Place as Gift, Promise and Challenge in Biblical Faith.* OBT. Philadelphia: Fortress/London:
SPCK, 1977, 1978.
"The study is organized around three histories of the land: a)
the history of promise into the *land*, b) the history of man-
agement into *exile*, and c) the new history of promise which
begins in exile and culminates in *kingdom*" (p. xv). Sweeping
in its scope; intended to help the church think through a vision
toward shalom.

482 N. C. Habel. *The Land Is Mine.* OBT. Minneapolis: Fortress, 1995.
Casts the discussion more in terms of ideology (six are noted,
e.g., royal ideology, theocratic ideology, immigrant ideology),
of which theology is often a component. Highlights the topic

of land rights and entitlement; takes account of current social, political, and religious debate.

9.18 Law

483 J. Levenson. "The Theologies of Commandment in Biblical Israel." *HTR* 73 (1980): 17–33.

In most theologies law is treated as part of covenant, a subordination of norm to narrative. Other paradigms such as the rational and cosmological need attention.

484 *'Gesetz' als thema Biblischer Theologie. JBTh* 4 (1989).

The entire issue of this annual is devoted to law. Articles pertinent to OT theology: law and gospel (W. H. Schmidt), commandment and law (N. Lohfink), law in priestly literature (M. Köckert).

485 O. Kaiser. "The Law as Center of the Hebrew Bible." Pp. 93–103 in *"Sha'arei Talmon": Studies in the Bible, Qumran, and the Ancient Near East Presented to Shemaryahu Talmon.* Edited by M. Fishbane, E. Tov with the assistance of W. W. Fields. Winona Lake, Ind.: Eisenbrauns, 1992.

Sees the covenantal concept as "the chief thread through the labyrinth of the Bible." Notes how redactional hints about the law in the prophetic books and elsewhere, as well as the structure of human existence given in the Pentateuch, point to a unity in the Hebrew Bible.

486 E. A. Martens. "Embracing the Law: A Biblical Theological Perspective." *BBR* 2 (1992): 1–28.

Expounds on three theses: (1) Torah as an expression of the will of God is good; (2) Torah functioned as an identity-marker for the OT people of God; and (3) when embraced in faith, Torah (though now superseded by Christ) was the vehicle for righteousness.

9.19 Messiah

487 G. Van Groningen. *Messianic Revelation in the Old Testament.* Grand Rapids: Baker, 1990.

A massive tome (1,018 pp.), the result of forty years of study by a staunch evangelical. After delineating the messianic concept, the author traces messianic revelation successively in the Pentateuch, Former Prophets, Poetic books, and Latter Prophets (one-half the book). Full indexes and bibliography.

488 W. C. Kaiser Jr. *The Messiah in the Old Testament.* SOTBT. Grand Rapids: Zondervan, 1995.

A well-known evangelical scholar exposits the topic largely by examining discrete texts. Presents a developing theme along the lines of the promise-plan from the Pentateuch through the historical and psalmnic literature to the prophets.

489 P. E. Satterwaite, R. S. Hess, and G. Wenham. *The Lord's Anointed: Interpretation of Old Testament Messianic Texts.* Grand Rapids: Baker/Carlisle: Paternoster, 1995.

Fourteen essays by as many writers canvassing the theme of "Messiah" via larger blocks, usually entire biblical books.

9.20 Mission

490 G. W. Peters. *A Biblical Theology of Missions.* Chicago: Moody, 1972.

Peters straddles the disciplines of bible exposition, theology, and mission. While the book is structured synthetically, significant sections (pp. 83–130) deal with the OT.

491 D. Senior and C. Stuhlmüller. *The Biblical Foundations for Mission.* Maryknoll, N.Y.: Orbis, 1983.

In the first half of the book Catholic Stuhlmüller deals with the OT, noting election and its ramifications for universalism and world salvation. Examines the prophetic challenge to acculturation and the prayers in the Psalms. Cf. synthesis in Part III. Helpfully laced with Scripture quotations.

492 W. A. Dyrness. *Let the Earth Rejoice! A Biblical Theology of Holistic Mission.* Westchester: Crossway, 1983.

To the question, "What is God's mission in the world?" Dyrness answers by examining four dramatic acts within the kingdom of God: (1) creation, (2) exodus, (3) exile, and (4) the event of Jesus Christ.

493 R. E. Hedlund. *The Mission of the Church to the World: A Biblical Theology.* Grand Rapids: Baker, 1991. Asian Edition: *Mission to Man in the Bible.* Madras: Evangelical Literature Service for Church Growth, 1985.

Expounds themes that speak to and define the mission of the church. Half the book deals with OT themes (e.g., universality in Genesis, election, liberation, the role of the nations, missionary psalms, and the prophetic method). Semipopular.

494 J. Goldingay and C. J. H. Wright. "'Yahweh Our God, Jahweh One.'" Pp. 34–52 in *One God, One Lord in a World of Religious Pluralism.* Edited by A. D. Clarke and B. W. Winter. Cambridge: Tyndale, 1991.

A survey on the teaching of the OT regarding other religions, noting exclusivist and universalist stances. At certain points the OT shows openness to other religions; at other times it does not because the risk would be too great.

495 C. H. H. Scobie. "Israel and the Nations: An Essay in Biblical Theology." *TynBul* 43 (1992): 283–305.

Israel related to the nations historically through incorporation, and eschatologically through an ingathering of the Gentiles. The latter is appropriated in the NT by Jesus and the early church. Helpful footnotes noting periodical articles on mission in the OT (p. 284).

9.21 Peace (See §9.29)

496 P. B. Yoder and W. M. Swartley (eds.). *The Meaning of Peace: Biblical Studies.* Studies in Peace and Scripture. Institute of Mennonite Studies. Translations by Walter Sawatsky. Louisville: Westminster/John Knox, 1992.

Essays, mostly previously published (e.g., C. Westermann) on OT (six essays) and NT (by, e.g., Luise Schottroff) on understandings of peace. Introductory essays and a major bibliography (18 pp.) by the editors.

9.22 Prayer

497 S. E. Balentine. *Prayer in the Hebrew Bible: The Drama of Divine–Human Dialogue.* OBT. Minneapolis: Fortress, 1993.

A thorough discussion of prose and nonpsalmic prayer in the OT, largely using a literary method. Explores depictions of both the pray-er and God, petition and praise, and the contribution of prayer material to the academic study of theology and to the life of the church. A focused non-clichéd work. Author and Scripture indexes; ample footnotes, but no bibliography.

498 P. D. Miller. *They Cried to the Lord: The Form and Theology of Biblical Prayer.* Minneapolis: Fortress, 1994.
Part II treats the genres of prayer (hymn, petition, thanksgiving, intercession); Part III, the sociological and theological understandings of prayer. An appendix offers structural outlines for forty-eight prayers. Heavily footnoted. A solid work; rich material.

9.23 Providence

499 J. Rogerson. "Can a Doctrine of Providence Be Based on the Old Testament?" Pp. 529–43 in *Ascribe to the Lord: Biblical and Other Studies in Memory of Peter C. Craigie.* Edited by Lyle Eslinger and Glen Taylor. JSOTSup 67. Sheffield: JSOT, 1988.
His answer: if OT writers believed that God controlled the destiny of a nation, Yes. If history was conceived by them as a process with a goal toward which God was guiding it, No (p. 542).

9.24 Righteousness (See §9.15)

9.25 Sacrifice

500 G. J. Wenham. "The Theology of Old Testament Sacrifice." Pp. 75–87 in *Sacrifice in the Bible.* Edited by R. T. Beckwith and M. J. Selman. Grand Rapids: Baker/Carlisle: Paternoster, 1995.
"The animal is a substitute for the worshipper. Its death makes atonement for the worshipper." The restoration of the worshiper to divine favor is common to the burnt, sin, and peace/fellowship offerings.

9.26 Salvation

501 T. V. Farris. *Mighty to Save: A Study in Old Testament Soteriology.* Nashville: Broadman, 1993.
A general but extensive overview working from stories (e.g., Eden, fall of Jericho), legislation (e.g., Day of Atonement), covenants, and analyses of certain texts. Intended for the pastor and general reader. No index or bibliography, but chapter endnotes point to sources.

9.27 Sin

502 R. P. Knierim. "On the Contours of Old Testament and Biblical Hamartiology." Pp. 416–67 in *The Task of Old Testament Theology* (#57).
Touches on method, traces concepts of sin, explains the resultant challenges to a coherent ontology, notes the Deity's critical involvement in culture, and compares the OT view of sin with that of the NT. Breaks new ground. Cf. his detailed study of the verbal roots for sin not only etymologically but contextually in *Die Hauptbegriffe für Sünde im Alten Testament.* Gütersloh: Gütersloher Verlagshaus Gerd Mohn, 1965.

9.28 Spirit of God/Spirituality

503 L. J. Wood. *The Holy Spirit in the Old Testament.* Grand Rapids: Zondervan, 1976.
Relates the work of the Spirit to creation, spiritual renewal, and the prophets. Holds that regeneration, indwelling, sealing, filling, and empowering by the Spirit were known in the OT. A relatively brief but responsible study.

504 R. Koch. *Der Geist Gottes im Alten Testament.* Frankfurt am Main: Peter Lang, 1991.
An influential Catholic theologian who has engaged in a half century of study on the topic emphasizes the work of the Spirit in conjunction with the Messiah, the community of the Mes-

siah, and the messianic time of salvation. Ecumenically sensitive; brief (140 pp.) but amply documented.

505 W. Hildebrandt. *An Old Testament Theology of the Spirit of God.* Peabody, Mass.: Hendrickson, 1995.
A much-expanded Regent College thesis begins with etymological matters, then proceeds synthetically to deal with the Spirit in creation, among God's people, in Israel's leadership, and in prophecy. Largely descriptive and often summary in nature. Balanced and helpful for initial exposure to the subject.

506 R. P. Knierim. "The Spirituality of the Old Testament." Pp. 269–97 in *The Task of the Old Testament* (#57).
Reconstructs the concept of spirituality but not with the customary lexical approach. Differentiates between a predisposition to spirituality and spirituality itself. Discusses the focus, expressions of, and source of OT spirituality.

9.29 War/Peace

507 P. C. Craigie. *The Problem of War in the Old Testament.* Grand Rapids: Eerdmans, 1978.
A slender volume but a helpful overview identifying components of the problem as God, revelation, and ethics. Each is analyzed for the lay reader; pointers toward resolutions are offered.

508 M. C. Lind. *Yahweh Is a Warrior: The Theology of Warfare in Ancient Israel.* Scottdale, Pa.: Herald, 1980.
A Mennonite scholar examines the Pentateuch and Deuteronomistic history, arguing that the paradigm for Yahweh war is the Exodus story: Yahweh was the sole Warrior. This principle also envisions a specific form of government. Vigorous interaction with other literature.

509 P. D. Hanson. "War and Peace in the Hebrew Bible." *Int* 38 (1984): 341–62.
Traces *shalom* within the sphere of worship, righteousness, and compassion through the OT. The opposite of *shalom* is chaos, not necessarily war.

510   G. von Rad. *Holy War in Ancient Israel*. Translated by Marva J.
Dawn. Grand Rapids: Eerdmans, 1991. Original Title: *Der Heilige
Krieg im alten Israel*. Göttingen: Vandenhoeck und Ruprecht.
Third Edition: 1958.

A description of the institution of Holy (or Yahweh) war from
the era of ancient Israel through the time of the prophets and
into Deuteronomy. B. C. Ollenburger offers a thirty-page inter-
pretive introduction and J. E. Sanders a thirty-page annotated
bibliography on "War, Peace and Justice in the Hebrew Bible:
A Representative Bibliography." A seminal work and basic
resource.

511   R. P. Knierim. "On the Subject of War in Old Testament and Biblical Theology." *HBT* 16 (1994): 1–19.

Interacts with an article by H. E. von Waldo, who claims that
"war is sin because it is a violation of God's order of creation"
(*HTR* 6.2 [1984]: 27–48). Knierim essentially agrees, but
nuances the position in view of God's alien work and the NT
perspective.

512   T. Longman III and D. G. Reid. *God Is a Warrior*. SOTBT. Grand
Rapids: Zondervan, 1995.

The divine warrior, described as a central biblical motif, is
traced by Longman through the OT (e.g., Day of the Lord, war-
ring against forces of chaos) and by Reid through the NT (e.g.,
Jesus and the exodus, new conquest, Paul and the Day of the
Lord, and holy warriors).

9.30 Worship (See §9.7)

Index of Modern Authors

Achtemeier, E., 70, 78, 105
Achtemeier, P., 78
Ackroyd, P. R., 15, 93, 100
Addinall, P., 40
Albertz, R., 45
Albrektson, B., 106
Allen, L. C., 102
Allen, R. J., 72
Allmen, J.-J von, 19
Alt, A., 79
Ammon, C. F. von, 73
Andersen, F. I., 122
Anderson, B. W., 18, 25, 28, 41, 62, 67, 116
Anderson, G. W., 15
Archer, G. L., 21
Armstrong, J. F., 103
Auld, A. G., 41

Baab, O., 76
Bailey, D. W., 108
Baker, D. L., 63
Balentine, S. E., 28, 117, 127
Baloian, B. E., 111
Barr, J., 17, 19, 28, 31, 32, 35, 40, 42, 44, 51, 52, 62, 71
Barth, C., 85
Barth, K., 44, 104
Barton, J. W., 28, 39, 120
Bauer, G. L., 61, 73

Bauer, J. B., 21
Baumgärtel, F., 18, 40, 50, 51, 62
Baumgarten-Crusius, L. F., 49
Beck, J. T., 51
Bell, R. D., 98
Bellinger, W. H., Jr., 116
Betz, O., 17
Beyreuther, E., 20
Bietenhard, H., 20
Birch, B. C., 48, 119
Blenkinsopp, J., 44, 67, 91
Bornemann, R., 41
Bosman, H. L., 49
Boström, L., 103
Botterweck, G. J., 20
Bowman, T., 35
Braun, R. L., 101
Brett, M. G., 86
Brettler, M. Z., 124
Bright, J., 70, 77, 113
Brocke, E., 68
Bromiley, G. W., 20
Brooke, G. J., 29, 67
Brown, C., 20
Brown, M. L., 122
Bruce, F. F., 80
Brueggemann, W., 18, 24, 26, 27, 28, 32, 33, 47, 69, 88, 92, 93, 101, 116, 124
Brunner, E., 25, 62

Bultmann, R., 25, 32, 62, 63
Burrows, M., 66, 75
Bush, F. W., 94

Carson, D. A., 25
Charlesworth, J. H., 66
Chestnut, J. S., 121
Childs, B. S., 17, 31, 32, 34, 35, 44, 46, 47, 48, 49, 54, 64, 65, 66, 69, 84, 86, 94, 96
Chisholm, R. B., Jr., 27, 91
Clements, R. E., 18, 26, 32, 46, 56, 81, 91, 92, 97
Clines, D. J. A., 89
Clowney, E. P., 70
Coats, G. W., 48, 96
Cobb, J. B., Jr., 51
Coenen, L., 20
Collins, J. J., 34, 41, 49, 52, 53
Cotterell, P., 19
Craigie, P. C., 130
Crenshaw, J. L., 92

Dalman, R., 16
Davidson, A. B., 31, 75
Davidson, R., 71, 79
Davies, G. H., 26
De Graaf, S. G., 81
De Vries, S. J., 83
Deissler, A., 80
Dentan, R. C., 38, 78
Dietrich, W., 59
Dillard, R. B., 94, 100
Dirksen, P., 44
Donahue, J. R., 24
Donner, H., 26
Dowd, S., 24
Drane, J., 84
Duke, R. K., 95
Dumbrell, W. J., 95, 112, 114
Durham, J. I., 26
Dyrness, W. A., 82, 126

Eades, K. L., 28
Ehlen, A. J., 51
Eichrodt, W., 18, 26, 28, 30, 31, 32, 38, 39, 43, 45, 46,47, 48, 49, 57, 62, 66, 69, 73, 76, 77, 78, 107, 111
Eissfeldt, O., 28, 31, 43
Elwell, W. A., 22
Engnell, I., 114
Exum, J. C., 98

Fabry, H. J., 20
Farris, T. V., 129
Fensham, F. C., 58
Ferch, A. J., 107
Finger, T., 45
Fiorenza, E., 69
Fishbane, M., 41
Fitzmyer, J. A., 15
Floyd, M. H., 28
Fohrer, G., 57, 80
Fosdick, H. E., 75
Fox, M., 101
Frei, H., 49
Fretheim, T. E., 88, 109, 121
Friedrich, G., 20
Fuller, D. P., 60

Gabler, J. P., 28, 32, 39, 42, 45, 47, 48, 49, 50
Gadamer, H. G., 65
Gaffin, R. B., Jr., 44
Gammie, J. G., 123
Garrett, D. A., 103, 104
Gese, H., 26, 32, 46, 63, 64, 65
Gilkey, L., 35, 50
Girdlestone, R. B., 19
Glanzman, G. S., 15
Gnuse, R., 34, 53
Goldingay, J., 14, 39, 55, 59, 71, 84, 97, 100, 120, 127
Goldsworthy, G., 82

Gorman, F. H., Jr., 89
Gorman, G. E., 16
Gorman, L., 16
Goshen-Gottstein, M., 41, 67
Gottwald, N. K., 26, 54, 106
Gous, I. G. P., 69
Gowan, D. E., 96, 118
Gray, J., 123
Gunkel, H., 17
Gunneweg, A. H. J., 52, 65, 86

Habel, N. C., 124
Hahn, H. F., 31
Hals, R. M., 98, 122
Hamilton, V. P., 96
Hanhart, R., 26
Hanks, T. D., 100
Hanson, P. D., 18, 24, 32, 39, 47,
  58, 84, 112, 130
Harrelson, W., 39, 97
Harrington, W. J., 38
Harris, R. L., 21
Hartley, J. H., 97
Hartley,. J. E., 101
Harvey, J., 33, 55
Hasel, G. F., 18, 27, 32, 33, 34,
  35, 37, 38, 44, 48, 50, 51, 58,
  64, 94, 105
Hattori, Y., 117
Hayes, J. H., 18, 33
Hedlund, R. E., 127
Heinisch, P., 77
Hempel, J., 17
Hengstenberg, E. W., 74
Herberg, W., 52
Hess, R. S., 126
Hesse, F., 40, 51
Hildebrandt, W., 130
Hoffman, Y., 123
Hofmann, J. C. K. von, 49, 50, 51
Høgenhaven, J., 40, 54
Holbert, J. C., 72

Houlden, J. H., 18
House, P. R., 99
Howie, C. G., 108
Hubbard, D. A., 26, 94
Hubbard, R. L., Jr., 27, 41, 114
Hübner, H., 34, 65
Hupper, W. G., 16

Irwin, W. A., 43

Jacob, E., 26, 31, 38, 57, 77
Janowski, B., 33, 58
Janzen, W., 120
Japhet, S., 100
Jenni, E., 22
Jeppsen, K., 44
Johnston, R. K., 27
Johnston, W., 100
Jones, G. H., 100

Kaiser, G. P., 49
Kaiser, O., 86, 125
Kaiser, W. C., Jr., 55, 58, 71, 81,
  119, 120, 126
Kapelrud, A. S., 114
Kaufman, G. D., 45
Keel, O., 104
Kelsey, D. H., 44
Kittel, G., 20, 85
Klein, G. L., 71
Klein, R. W., 93, 105
Knierim, R. P., 28, 39, 45, 49, 54,
  67, 97, 116, 129, 130, 131
Knight, G. A. F., 26, 78
Koch, R., 129
Köckert, M., 125
Köhler, L., 18, 62, 77
Kraeling, E. G., 44, 62
Kraftchick, S. J., 28, 35
Kräsovec, J., 123
Kraus, H.-J., 63, 102
Kutsch, E., 114

Labuschagne, C. J., 120
Ladd, G. E., 17
LaSor, W. S., 94
Laurin, R. B., 26
Lehman, C. K., 76, 80
Lemche, N. P., 53
Lemke, W. E., 53
Lemke, W., 18
Lempke, H., 41
Léon-Dufour, X., 20
Levenson, J., 41, 68, 84, 125
Limburg, J., 71
Lind, M. C., 130
Loewen, H. J., 45
Lohfink, N., 24, 70, 82, 90, 115, 125
Lonergan, B., 47
Long, B. O., 29
Longman, T., III, 25, 94, 131
Luc, A., 107

Manaham, R. E., 106
Martens, E. A., 27, 29, 35, 45, 53, 82, 95, 125
Marti, K., 34
Martin, J. A., 99
Mauser, U., 23, 24, 53
Mayo, S. M., 71
Mays, J. L., 26, 102, 109
McCann, J. C., Jr., 102
McCarthy, D. J., 113
McComiskey, T. E., 114
McConville, J. G., 59, 90, 97
McCurley, F. R., 84
McEvenue, S. E., 47
McFague, S., 54
McKeating, H., 107
McKenzie, J. L., 25, 62, 81
Merrill, E. H., 27, 89, 107
Mettinger, T. N. D., 122
Meye, R. P., 27
Middleton, J. R., 116

Milazzo, G. T., 117
Miller, P. D., 28, 90, 91, 128
Minear, P., 35
Miranda, J. P., 68
Miskotte, K. H., 70
Moberly, R. W. L., 42, 89
Moller, G. I., 28
Morus, S. F. N., 45
Muilenburg, J., 119
Müller, H.-P., 113
Murphy, R. E., 29, 39, 56, 62, 103, 104
Murray, J., 44
Murray, R., 115
Myers, C. D., Jr., 28

Nelson, R. D., 117
Nesbit, W. G., 46
Nicholson, E. W., 114
Niehaus, J. J., 86
North, C. R., 43
North, R., 16, 99
Noth, M., 114

O'Connor, K. M., 28, 92
Och, B., 117
Oehler, G. F., 30, 74
Oeming, M., 65
Ollenburger, B. C., 17, 27, 28, 39, 45, 49, 117, 124, 131
Olson, D. T., 98
Ortlund, R. C., Jr., 25
Oswalt, J. N., 105
Otto, E., 120
Overholt, T. W., 106

Pannenberg, W., 29, 51
Parke-Taylor, G. H., 121
Patrick, D., 121
Payne, J. B., 79
Pedersen, S., 66
Penchansky, D., 35

Perdue, L. G., 54, 92
Perlitt, L., 114
Peters, G. W., 126
Petersen, D. L., 26
Pitkin, R. E., 20
Plöger, O., 118
Pokorny, P., 42
Porteous, N. W., 18, 31
Pressler, C. J., 69
Preuss, H. D., 87, 118
Priest, J. F., 54
Prinsloo, G. T. M., 72
Prinsloo, W. S., 99
Procksch, O., 26, 40, 62, 76
Prussner, F. C., 33, 57

Rad, G. von, 17, 18, 26, 31, 32, 34, 38, 39, 40, 45, 46, 47, 48, 50, 52, 54, 55, 56, 57, 58, 59, 62, 63, 65, 66, 76, 79, 90, 91, 115, 131
Rahner, K., 49
Raitt, T. M., 93
Reid, D. G., 131
Reimer, A. J., 45
Rendtorff, R., 28, 36, 41, 51, 67, 68, 91, 115, 116
Reumann, J., 26, 34, 61, 84
Reventlow, H. G., 19, 33, 35, 39, 59, 62, 65, 123
Richards, L. O., 21
Richardson, A., 19, 25, 62
Ringgren, H., 20
Roberts, J. J. M., 93, 105
Robertson, O. P., 109, 113
Robinson, H. W., 75
Robinson, J. M., 28, 51
Robinson, R. B., 49
Rogerson, J., 128
Rowley, H. H., 14, 35, 57
Ruether, R., 69
Rust, E. C., 91

Sabourin, L., 23, 64
Saebø, M., 24
Sailhamer, J. H., 89
Sakenfeld, K. D., 122
Salters, R. B., 106, 109
Sanders, J. A., 33, 66
Sanders, J. E., 131
Satterwaite, P. E., 126
Schedl, C., 84
Schertz, M., 45
Schmidt, H. H., 55, 116
Schmidt, W. H., 24, 32, 59, 83, 125
Schofield, J. N., 26, 79
Schottroff, L., 127
Schreiner, J., 87
Schultz, H., 32, 74
Schultz, R., 50
Scobie, C. H. H., 55, 56, 66, 127
Seebass, H., 59, 64, 65, 66, 83
Seitz, C., 24
Sellin, E., 57, 62, 75
Selman, M. J., 124
Senior, D., 126
Sheppard, G. T., 102
Smart, J. D., 30, 32, 43
Smend, R., 26, 34, 57
Smick, E., 47
Smith, G. V., 56, 108
Smith, R. L., 34, 86, 107, 108, 109, 110
Snaith, N. H., 123
Spriggs, D. G., 46
Stade, B., 34
Stendahl, K., 17, 48
Stier, F., 15
Strange, J., 53
Strom, M., 85
Stuhlmacher, P., 58, 64, 65, 96
Stuhlmüller, C., 105, 126
Sun, H. T. C., 28
Swartley, W. M., 127
Sweeney, M. A., 29, 68

Tate, M. E., 32
Terrien, S., 32, 33, 46, 47, 54, 55, 64, 66, 81, 112
Thompson, J. A., 106
Towner, W. S., 39
Trible, P., 48, 49, 69, 121
Tsevat, M., 41, 67
Tucker, G. M., 26, 44

Unger, M. F., 21

Van Gemeren, W. A., 22, 25, 85, 94
Van Groningen, G., 125
Van Heerden, S. W., 49
Van Imschoot, P., 26, 79
Van Ruler, A. A., 63
Vatke, J. K., 49
Vaux, R. de, 38, 52
Vawter, B., 15
Vischer, W., 63, 76
Vogels, W., 113
Vos, G., 44, 76, 80
Vriezen, T. C., 18, 25, 26, 38, 46, 57, 77, 104, 118

Waldo, H. E. von, 131
Walker-Jones, A. W., 48
Waltke, B. K., 21, 103
Walton, J. H., 115
Ward, W. E., 47

Watts, J. D. W., 89, 105
Weber, H.-R., 85
Weber, M., 58, 114
Wenham, G. J., 98, 126, 128
Wessels, W. J., 48, 66
Westermann, C., 22, 25, 29, 32, 46, 47, 51, 54, 62, 64, 65, 71, 83, 106, 113, 121, 127
Wette, W. M. L. de, 49
White, W., 21
Whybray, R. N., 40
Williams, D. L., 108
Williamson, H. G. M., 101
Wilson, R. R., 26
Wolff, H. W., 26, 69, 88, 90, 112
Wood, L. J., 129
Woudstra, M. H., 98
Wright, C. J. H., 127
Wright, G. E., 18, 35, 46, 50, 51, 52, 54, 62, 76, 119, 120
Wurthwein, E., 33
Wyrtzen, D. B., 107

Yoder, P. B., 127
Young, E. J., 31, 38
Youngblood, R., 80

Zannoni, A. E., 16
Zimmerli, W., 17, 18, 25, 34, 48, 55, 58, 62, 64, 82, 118, 121
Zuck, R. B., 27, 96

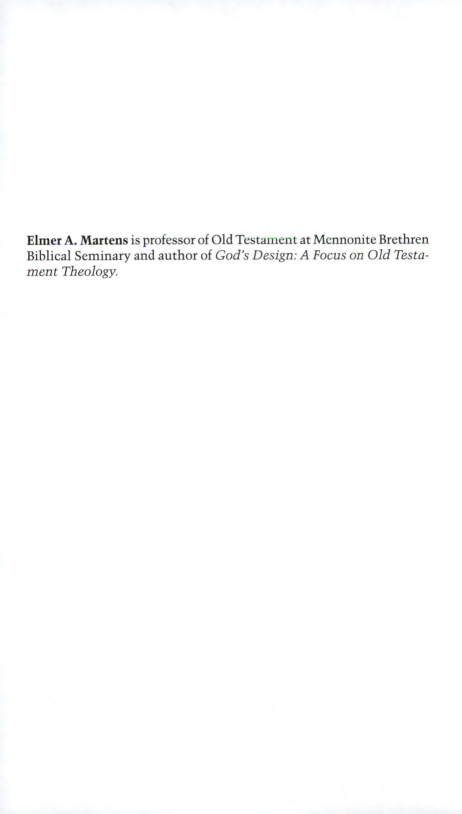

Elmer A. Martens is professor of Old Testament at Mennonite Brethren Biblical Seminary and author of *God's Design: A Focus on Old Testament Theology.*